LOVING MESSY PEOPLE

Loving *Messy* People

The Messy Art of Helping One Another Become More Like Jesus

Shepherd Press
Wapwallopen, Pennsylvania

Loving Messy People

© 2020 Scott Mehl

ISBN
Paper: 978-1-63342-183-7
epub: 978-1-63342-184-4
Kindle: 978-1-63342-185-1

Shepherd Press
P.O. Box 24
Wapwallopen, PA 18660

www.shepherdpress.com

Cover design by Jacy Corral
Page design by **documen**. www.documen.co.uk
Printed in the USA

APPRECIATION FOR *LOVING MESSY PEOPLE*

Rich in stories, practical in application, pastoral in tone, and crisp in content, *Loving Messy People* draws our gaze towards the reality of human messiness with a full mind and a fresh voice. In these pages we discover that the disordered life we all inhabit responds and flourishes under *gospel care*—the grace-saturated, cross-empowered love that emerges within a soul and community as they become more like Jesus. If you're like me and need help with your messy life, or you just want to help others to take simple steps forward out of chaos, buy and give away *Loving Messy People*.

Dave Harvey
President of Great Commission Collective
Founder of AmICalled.com
Author of *When Sinners Say I Do, Rescuing Ambition,*
and *I Still Do*

Some people may look at the church and assume (wrongly) that Christians are people who have it all together. But the truth is that Christians are people who know, first of all, that they don't have it together—that they are in need of a Savior. Scott Mehl knows that's true because he's been a pastor who has lived life with messy people, but he also knows it because he knows himself. He knows he's a mess, too, and so he brings to the care of people practical answers that really do help and a love for the gospel that alone has the power to transform lives. If you want to help messy people, or if you are one, then this book is for you.

Elyse M Fitzpatrick
Author of *Counsel from the Cross*

In a culture where people usually bail when relationships get difficult, the church desperately needs to learn how to embrace the mess and experience the very depth of community for which we were made. In *Loving Messy People*, Scott Mehl proves to be a helpful guide. With theological insight and practical tools, Mehl teaches how to love people the way Jesus did so we can become the people Jesus made us to be. I hope this book gets read widely.

Jeremy Treat
Pastor for Preaching and Vision at Reality LA in Los Angeles, California
Adjunct Professor of Theology at Biola University
Author of *Seek First* and *The Crucified King*

The gospel of Jesus Christ radically saves and sanctifies us, bringing us into real relationship with God and with one another. Through the gospel, God creates a gospel community— the church—and calls us to love one another like Jesus. The problem is that loving messy people is hard. And we're not Jesus. But God is good. Our Lord empowers and equips everyone he calls through the power of the gospel.

Loving Messy People is a biblical treasure chest of encouragement, hope, pastoral wisdom, and practical instruction that brings the gospel to life and enables the reader to not only discover and learn but actually implement and reproduce gospel care and love. It is an essential tool for any pastor or Christian looking to effectively and biblically love and serve others in the power and likeness of Jesus Christ. Scott Mehl puts the gospel in "3-D, high definition sound" by providing the church with a redemptive framework and playbook for gospel love in action. I highly recommend this book for any Christian seeking to apply the radical, life-changing love of the gospel to the messy lives around them.

Ryan Townsend
Executive Director, 9Marks

This important book is a much-needed manual for equipping every Christian (not just pastors and professional counselors) to fulfill the call of Romans 15:14 to help one another to grow to become more like Jesus.

Mehl draws on a wealth of pastoral experience as he shows the reader how to use biblical principles to care for people in very realistic (and messy) life situations. As the title indicates, soul care is "messy." There isn't a ten-step formula which will solve every problem. Rather, we lovingly listen and then speak the truth to hurting people and then stand back and see the great things that God can do through his powerful Word."

Jim Newheiser
Associate Professor of Pastoral Theology and the Director of the Christian Counseling Program, Reformed Theological Seminary, Charlotte
Executive Director, IBCD (The Institute for Biblical Counseling and Discipleship)
Author of *Money: Seeking God's Kingdom; Marriage, Divorce, and Remarriage*

Messiness is a common denominator in all of our lives. In *Loving Messy People*, Mehl leans in close in order to encourage us in gospel truth, pastorally confronting us with kindness and pointing to the hope of change found in the sure work of Jesus. Mehl seeks to remove our fears and hesitations to engage in the messy lives of others, knowing the goal is not to remain sanitary but to be sanctified as we serve Christ by serving others.

Dale Johnson
Executive Director, Association of Certified Biblical Counselors
Associate Professor of Biblical Counseling, Midwestern Baptist Theological Seminary

Scott Mehl has written a creative and easy-to-digest work that will help motivate and equip *all* believers in their God-given role of ministry to one another. He has gone into more detail than many biblical counseling resources on how anyone can apply scriptural principles in a relational model of "gospel care." Scott's chapter on love (and its overarching role in helping others) is one of the best I've read on the subject and is immensely practical. In addition, Scott consistently ties everyday ministry to Jesus, the gospel, and being conformed to his image. If you are looking for a helpful resource for where to begin in following Christ in your ministry to other believers who are struggling, you have found it.

Stuart Scott
Professor of Biblical Counseling, The Masters University
Author of *The Exemplary Husband* and *The Faithful Parent*

There is no more formidable tool in the hand of God than a broken person ministering the grace of Jesus Christ to another broken person over the long haul, yet we often shy away from such ministry because of laziness, selfishness, or fear. Enter Scott Mehl's *Loving Messy People*, an immensely encouraging book full of scriptural insights examined in the context of real-life examples. These insights will give you a realistic picture of what you can expect to encounter in your relationships with other believers, a more hopeful vision of what church community can be like, and an uplifting perspective on how you can become a fully-engaged participant in this slow-motion miracle we call sanctification.

Milton Vincent
Pastor-Teacher, Cornerstone Fellowship Bible Church in Riverside, CA
Author of *A Gospel Primer for Christians*

The Bible calls us to love one another as Christ has loved us—us messy sinners. I am one of them, and so are you, so let's all praise the Lord! Grace abounds. If we are going to be faithful disciples of the risen Christ, then we, too, must love the messy sinners in our lives. With real stories, pastoral wisdom, and piercing application of the gospel, Scott helps us see how the Good News gives us a framework and a fire in our bones to love one another like Christ loves us.

J.A. Medders
Pastor of Preaching and Theology, Redeemer Church in Tomball, TX
Author of *Humble Calvinism*

Loving others is a difficult but necessary pathway to our joy in Jesus. Situations are complex. People are not always receptive. We don't know what to say or if it will really help. Dr. Mehl teaches us to love by knowing, serving, speaking, and "gospeling." As a pastor responsible for equipping my people to speak the truth in love to one another, this is now my go-to book recommendation. *Loving Messy People* simplifies love for others in complex situations so that you confidently do your part in helping them find true happiness in Jesus.

P. J. Tibayan
Member and Pastor-Theologian, Bethany Baptist Church in Bellflower, California

I am so thankful for the ministry of Scott Mehl. A faithful man, husband, father, and Christian. He is a reliable shepherd and a trustworthy voice.

Heath Lambert
Senior Pastor, First Baptist Church of Jacksonville, FL
Author of *Finally Free* and *A Theology of Biblical Counseling*

DEDICATION

To My Spiritual Family
Cornerstone Church of West L.A.

*Now concerning brotherly love you have no need
for anyone to write to you, for you yourselves have
been taught by God to love one another, for that
indeed is what you are doing to all the brothers [and
sisters] throughout [Los Angeles]. But we urge you,
brothers [and sisters], to do this more and more.*
(1 Thessalonians 4:9-10)

Contents

Chapter 1   Called into the Mess   15

Chapter 2   The Goal and the Gospel   27

Chapter 3   The Unscripted Art of Gospel Care   39

Chapter 4   The Melody of Love   51

Knowing

Chapter 5   An Intelligent Heart   65

Chapter 6   What's Most Needed?   79

Serving

Chapter 7   More Than a Counselor   93

Chapter 8   When the Mess Spills on You   107

Speaking

Chapter 9   Strength for Today and Bright Hope
             for Tomorrow   121

Chapter 10   More Than a Friend   135

Gospeling

Chapter 11   The Mess Outside of Us   147

Chapter 12   The Mess Inside of Us   163

Chapter 13   Tell Me the Old, Old Story   179

Chapter 14   More Than Change   195

Chapter 15   The Simplicity of Unscripted Love   211

             Acknowledgments   217

CHAPTER 1

CALLED INTO THE *Mess*

L ife is messy. Your life is messy. Your friends' lives are messy. Your small-group leader's life is messy. Your pastor's life is messy. Being messy is one of the hallmarks of being human. Every person you know has a messy life. And becoming a Christian doesn't change that.

The first time I realized this was in college. When God grabbed ahold of my life I quickly found myself surrounded by Christians. But these weren't the perfect Christians you see smiling on church websites. I was surrounded by people who believed firmly in the gospel and loved Jesus passionately, yet many of them were still hurting, struggling with sin, doubting, or confused. I was surrounded by messy people with messy lives. I didn't know exactly what they needed, and I didn't know what I had to offer. But I knew that God wanted me to play some part in their stories.

The first time I led a small group as a part of our local church something similar happened. I was excited about the potential of the young men I had invited. They had committed to study Scripture and live life together in a way they never had before. But as we dug into one another's lives it became obvious that many of these guys were also hurting, struggling with sin, doubting, or confused. I was again surrounded by messy people with messy lives. I didn't know exactly what they needed, and I didn't know what I had to offer. But again I knew that God wanted me to play some part in their stories.

I am sure you can imagine what happened when my wife and I moved to West Los Angeles to plant a church. God began drawing people to our young church, new believers coming to faith and established believers committing to reach our city. As our core group formed and relationships deepened, I was able to see how each one of the members of our brand-new church was hurting, struggling with sin, doubting, or confused as well. I was *again* surrounded by messy people with messy lives. I didn't *know* exactly what they needed, and I wasn't sure what I had to offer. But *again*, I knew that God wanted me to play some part in their stories.

Even now, after pastoring that same church for over a decade, I think about the community group that meets at our house every Friday night. These are some of our closest friends. Our kids play sports together, we hang out late on our back patio together, and we share our lives with one another. And you know what? They're all pretty messy. Some of them are hurting, struggling with sin, doubting, or confused, too. And sometimes I'm still not exactly sure what they need, and sometimes I still wonder what I have to offer. But I *know* that God wants me to play some part in their stories.

My entire life I have been surrounded by messy people with messy lives. The only reason it doesn't bother me is because I'm messy, too. And not like drippy burrito messy, but more like swimming in salsa messy. I'm sure my friends look at me and wonder to themselves, "Why do I always end up around people like this?" Do you ever find yourself asking that question? Maybe you wonder, "Is there something wrong with me that I keep attracting people with messy lives?" Or you begin to strategize, "If I could just find some non-messy people to befriend, I might finally have some uncomplicated relationships!"

But it should be familiar to be around messy people. That's what the church is. I assume that's been your experience, too. Some people can trick you for a season, but I promise, they're just as messy as the rest of us. All Christians are. Eventually the depression, anxiety, chronic health issues, addictions, doubts, insecurities, pride, abuse, prejudice, or poverty will come to the surface. To know a person is to know their mess.

Maybe you have a friend who has confessed her struggle with eating to you. She desires to be disciplined and knows what she *should* do, but she just can't seem to resist her constant cravings. Maybe there's a younger man at church who has asked you for help because he's completely unmotivated at work and is afraid his poor performance is going to cost him his job. Maybe your daughter is plagued by panic attacks or your son is beginning to wonder if God made a mistake creating him physically male. Whatever the stories are in your life, I'm sure you've wondered (possibly even in a panicked tone), "Oh man! What do I say? What do I do? Where do I turn?"

So, what *does* it look like to be a part of God's story written in the mess? How does God plan to address the hurt, sin, and confusion in the lives of your friends and family? What do you really have to offer those around you? How will God deal with all this mess?

Well, God deals with the mess using a beautiful amalgamation of means. God has dealt with the mess eternally by sending his Son to die on the cross and conquer sin and death. He has sent ongoing provision for the mess in the form of his Spirit. He has given us clear and sufficient truth in the midst of the mess through his Word. But the primary way God intends to deliver the message of his Son, as communicated in his Word and empowered by his Spirit, is you. *You* are God's provision. *You* are a central part of God's story of redemption and sanctification of those around you. Yes, you. Even with all your mess.

Your mess doesn't disqualify you from being used by God. In fact, it makes you even more qualified. God loves using messy people to minister to messy people. If he used clean and shiny people, they would receive all the glory. But God loves using people like you and me so that there is no doubt who gets credit for the work he does. "But we have this treasure in jars of clay, to show that the surpassing power belongs to God and not to us" (2 Cor. 4:7).

This is the point Paul Tripp makes in his classic book *Instruments in the Redeemer's Hands*:

> *Many of us would be relieved if God had placed our sanctification in the hands of trained and paid professionals, but that simply is not the biblical model. God's plan is that through the faithful ministry of every part, the whole body will grow to full maturity in Christ. The leaders of his church have been gifted, positioned, and appointed to train and mobilize the people of God for this "every person, every day" ministry lifestyle.* [1]

Tripp's vocabulary is from Ephesians 4:11–16. The apostle Paul describes God's desire to use us in one another's mess. He combines the example of Christ, God's design of the church, and the work of the Holy Spirit to clearly describe God's call on each one of us to this lifestyle of personal ministry.

SPEAKING THE TRUTH IN LOVE

> *And he gave the apostles, the prophets, the evangelists, the shepherds and teachers, to equip the saints for the work of ministry, for building up the body of Christ, until we all attain to the unity of the faith and of the knowledge of the Son of God, to mature manhood, to the measure of the stature of the fullness of Christ, so that we may no longer be children, tossed to and fro by the waves and carried about by every wind of doctrine, by human cunning, by craftiness in deceitful schemes. Rather, speaking the truth in love, we are to grow up in every way into him who is the head, into Christ, from whom the whole body, joined and held together by every joint with which it is equipped, when each part is working properly, makes the body grow so that it builds itself up in love.*
>
> *(Eph. 4:11–16)*

Whatever the cause of the mess, God has a plan to help each one of us grow. And at the center of his plan he has placed you and me. I am called to speak the truth to you in the midst of your mess. You are called to speak the truth to me in the midst of my mess. This is not just the calling of pastors, missionaries, counselors, or Bible study leaders; if you are a Christian, this is your calling, too. God wants to use *you*, even in the midst of your mess, to speak loving truth into the lives of other messy people.

But for us to live out God's call to minister in the midst of the mess, both truth and love are necessary. Loving someone without truth is like being a bad Uber driver. It's like being a driver who is meticulous about the comfort of his passengers, but doesn't have any navigation skills or knowledge of the city he's driving in. You make sure the temperature in the car is just right. You put on your passenger's favorite music. You provide them with a plethora of phone-charging cords, and offer gum or candy for the trip. But then you spend thirty minutes simply wandering around the streets of the city and end up dropping off your passenger miles from where they actually need to go.

Similarly, when we fall into the trap of loving others without speaking truth, we end up wandering aimlessly. This is what happens when we are kind, polite, caring, and compassionate, but fail to bring the truth of God and the gospel to bear when a person is struggling. The truth of God and the message of the gospel are the only things that can provide true hope, peace, joy, and transformation in the midst of our messes. To act lovingly toward someone but withhold what they desperately need isn't real love. We cannot build one another up through niceness or well wishes. We must love one another enough to courageously and wisely speak the truth.

On the other hand, speaking truth without love can also be compared to being a bad Uber driver, just in a different way. It's like being a driver who knows exactly where to go but has no interest in his passenger's safety or comfort. You pick up your passenger in your beat-up 1973 Ranchero that is filled to the roof with fast-food garbage so they have to sit in the open back with no seats and no seat belts. Your passenger hops in, only to find a coyote carcass and a month's supply of beer cans, while you take off racing down the street and squealing your tires around every turn. When you arrive at their destination you discover that your passenger hopped out miles ago at a stoplight because it was all too much. You may have arrived at the destination, but you failed to bring your passenger along with you.

This is what it's like when we throw our favorite Bible verses at people without considering whether they are actually what is most needed. Too many people have been convinced that biblical truth "doesn't work," not because there was a problem with the truth, but because the truth wasn't communicated with love. It may be true that "all things work together for good, for those who are called according to his purpose" (Rom. 8:28), but is that verse what is most needed or the best application of love in every moment of every mess? Oftentimes not.

This also happens when we speak truth but don't demonstrate that truth through our sacrificial actions. Messy people need more than just truth spoken to them. They need it lived out for them. I think this is partially why the phrase translated "speaking the truth" in Ephesians 4:15 is actually only one word in the original language: "truthing." Paul's call is literally for us to be "truthing" one another in love. While this undeniably includes speaking the truth, it also involves much more.

As we'll see throughout this book, the call to "truth" one another in love is everywhere in Scripture, and it should be everywhere in our lives. No matter what the circumstances or cause of the mess, you and I have much to offer the messy people all around us.

COMFORTING IN THE MESS OF SUFFERING

Sometimes a person's mess comes from someone or somewhere else. We live in a horribly fallen world where our fallen friends and family, fallen coworkers and neighbors, fallen environment, fallen bodies, and fallen culture all compound to create quite a mess. We suffer every day under the effects of this fallenness, and so does everyone around us. This is why God calls us to comfort one another in the midst of the mess: "Blessed be the God and Father of our Lord Jesus Christ, the Father of mercies and God of all comfort, who comforts us in all our affliction, so that we may be able to comfort those who are in any affliction, with the comfort with which we ourselves are comforted by God" (2 Cor. 1:3-4).

God comforts us in our mess. As the psalmist wrote, "This is my comfort in my affliction, that your promise gives me life" (Ps. 119:50). Or as Jesus said, "Come to me, all who labor and are heavy laden, and I will give you rest" (Matt. 11:28). But God's comfort, as beautiful and sustaining as it is, was never meant to find its end in you or me alone. God comforts us for a reason beyond our own contentment: so that we "may be able to comfort those who are in any affliction." God blesses us so that we may be a blessing.

This means that when those around you are suffering, it's not up to them to find comfort on their own. You and I are called to be God's agents of comfort to those around us. God has placed you in the lives of suffering people so that they may be comforted by you with the same comfort you have been comforted with by God. "Truthing" in love means coming alongside those who are hurting and speaking the glorious, hope-giving, life-sustaining truth of God and the gospel. Whether they are suffering from abuse, sickness, discouragement, depression, homelessness, or discrimination, we are each called to deliver God's hope to the hurting.

Restoring in the Mess of Sin

Sometimes a person's mess comes from within. We are all sinners desperately in need of grace, and becoming a Christian doesn't erase that need. Our hearts still chase after lesser loves and our flesh still cries out for selfish desires. And more often than any of us would care to admit, we give in. Our sin reveals itself in many different ways, from the obvious (porn, lying, drug abuse, etc.) to the more subtle (workaholism, quiet anger, escaping through entertainment, etc.). But just as God calls us to speak into one another's suffering, he calls us to speak into one another's sin as well: "Brothers, if anyone is caught in any transgression, you who are spiritual should restore him in a spirit of gentleness" (Gal. 6:1).

You may read this and see the "out" you've been looking for when Paul writes that it is the "spiritual" who are called to restore their brother or sister. This is the responsibility of "spiritual" Christians, not "normal" Christians like you, right? Wrong. Just before this passage, at the end of Galatians 5, we find the list of the fruit of the Spirit. This is the fruit that is naturally being produced in the lives of *everyone* who has the Holy Spirit inside them. So, if you have the Holy Spirit living inside you, you are the "spiritual" Christian Paul is referring to. And it is *your* responsibility to restore *any* of your brothers or sisters who are caught in sin.

When those around you are caught in sin, it's not up to them to find the way out on their own. You and I are called to be God's agents of restoration in their lives. God has placed you in the lives of sinning people so that they may be restored to him through your gentle, careful, sacrificial love. "Truthing" in love means speaking the glorious, hope-giving, life-sustaining truth of God and the gospel to those who are caught in sin. Whether their sin comes in the form of addiction, laziness, covetousness, murder, pride, or lust, we are each called to deliver God's restoration in the mess of sin.

WHAT'S GETTING IN THE WAY?

We are all called to minister to one another and build one another up. We are all called to care for one another in the mess of suffering. We are all called to restore one another in the mess of sin. But if the biblical call to minister to one another is so clear, what's holding us back? What keeps us from fully engaging in the lives of those around us in the way God has designed? Why do we all seem to find this kind of personal ministry so difficult?

There are probably messy people in your life right now who have come to mind as you've read this chapter. What is keeping you from comforting them in the midst of their suffering or restoring them in the midst of their sin? Of course, I can't answer these questions for you specifically. But I *can* identify a few of the barriers that I often hear, and briefly tell you how I hope this book will help.

BUSYNESS

We're all busy. There are only twenty-four hours in a day, and somehow we seem to spend every single one of them. Jerry Bridges lamented that "We are all so busy, absorbed in our own responsibilities and insulated from one another. We pass each other like ships in the night."[2] While I don't think this book will make you any less busy, my prayer is that it will help clarify what you ought to be busy doing. I don't want to simply add one more expectation to your plate, but instead help you see how much personal ministry you are already doing in the midst of your busy schedule, and empower you to be even more effective with the limited time that you have.

SELF-FOCUS

When I say that we are all called to comfort, restore, and minister to one another, I'm afraid that what you hear is "Someone should be comforting, restoring, and ministering to me!" I often hear people say something to the effect of, "That sounds so great! I just wish someone would do that for me." My hope is that this book will help you see how completely God *has* loved you and provided for you, and that it will encourage you to take your eyes off of yourself in order to see the opportunities to love others. We all know how *we* want to be loved; this book is about how we learn to love our neighbors as ourselves.

Trellis Work

In their insightful book *The Trellis and the Vine*, Colin Marshall and Tony Payne divide the work we traditionally refer to as "ministry" into two categories: trellis work and vine work.[3] Trellis work is the running of programs, serving on committees, and the maintaining of the institutional structure of the church. Vine work is the personal caring for and nurturing of souls. The goal of a trellis is to provide a structure upon which a vine can grow. The trellis is important, but only to the extent that it serves and facilitates the growth of the vine. What Ephesians 4 calls all of us to is vine work: the nurturing, comforting, and restoring of one another in love. Sometimes we can get distracted by all the important trellis work needed in the church and can view our planning of events, serving on committees, or setting up for a Sunday service as our contribution to the church. But, while trellis work has its place, we can't miss the fact that every one of us is called to vine work as well. Vine work is what this book is designed to equip you for.

Lack of Equipping

A desire to be equipped may have been the reason you picked this book up in the first place. You may feel like you don't know what to say, what to do, or where to start when it comes to the messes around you. You may feel that you don't have enough knowledge of people or the Bible to really minister effectively in the midst of someone else's mess. My hope is that this book will help in that department, but of course it won't provide all the equipping you need. One of the best resources I can encourage you to turn to is your pastor. All the pastors I know would *love* for someone in their church to come to them and ask to learn more about how to help others. And if your pastor doesn't know where to begin (or if you're a pastor yourself), maybe reading through this book together would be a great place to start.

LACK OF CONFIDENCE

I am convinced that the single biggest hindrance to personal ministry in the church today is a lack of confidence—lack of confidence in the Word of God as sufficient for all of life; lack of confidence in the Spirit of God to actually change people; lack of confidence in our own Spirit-empowered ability to help people in the midst of their mess. More than anything else, my prayer is that this book will help address the lack of confidence that I know you feel. As we look at how Scripture gives us guidance for every aspect of our relationships, I pray that you will become more confident that the Word of God truly is sufficient for even the messiest situations you will ever face. As we meditate on the power of the gospel to truly transform people, I pray that you will become more confident in the work of the Spirit. And as we learn about the art of ministering to one another, I pray that you will become more confident in your own Spirit-empowered ability, and realize just how much faithful ministry you are already doing.

WHAT ABOUT YOU?

The church where I am privileged to pastor is filled with people just like you who experience barriers just like yours. They're busy, they can be selfish, they get distracted by trellis work, they need to be equipped, and they lack confidence. Yet many of them have heard God's call to speak the truth in love to one another and are seeing God work in incredible ways in the midst of the mess. None of them are doing it perfectly, but that's the beauty of it. Just like you, they are just messy people surrounded by other messy people. God is working through them, and, sometimes, even in spite of them.

Amy is a work-at-home mom. Her life is packed with kids' needs and activities. Her husband is a huge blessing, but he works long hours. Amy is often on her own caring for their three kids as well as the occasional foster child. Amy's first passion is to disciple her children, but beyond that there are others in her life who look to her for help and guidance as well. Old acquaintances, moms in her community group, and other friends all have messy lives. Sometimes Amy doesn't know where to start, but she recognizes God's call for her to be a speaker of truth in love. So she faithfully ministers to those around her, whether it's through a short conversation at the park or via text message.

Abe is a young single professional. There are innumerable opportunities in West LA for a young single person like him. Almost any lifestyle he would want is at his fingertips. Yet Abe has committed his life to serving and loving other people even while maintaining his professional career. Instead of spending his free time on himself, he often spends it serving and speaking the truth in love to his brothers and sisters in Christ. Instead of simply seeking to be entertained or distracted, he uses this season in his life as a unique opportunity to bless and love others.

Nancy is a trained therapist. She has enough training to open her own practice, but her real passion is simply to volunteer as a part of the church family. She loves to speak the truth in love to her brothers and sisters who find themselves in particularly messy situations. She has found her training helpful, but she knows that only the gospel can actually transform hearts. So she dedicates much of her free time and energy to ministering in the context of the local church.

Brian is a gifted preacher. His communication gifts have been affirmed ever since he was in college. He's the kind of pastor who could have settled into a role as a "teaching pastor" and spent the vast majority of his time studying, preaching, and simply interacting with church staff. But God's conviction on Brian's heart to truly shepherd people has led him to develop into a gifted discipler as well. He has become someone who speaks the truth in love privately as well as publicly, and who regularly serves those in his community as a fellow brother in Christ.

Jenni is a new believer. Well, she's not now, but she was when she began ministering to others. When the gospel grabbed ahold of Jenni's life, it wasn't long before God gave her opportunities to speak the beauty of that truth into others' lives as well. Early on in her walk with Christ, Jenni realized that the hope and truth she had been given were not just for her. God had redeemed her for a purpose, and even with her limited biblical knowledge she still had the opportunity (and responsibility) to bless others with whatever knowledge she had.

Dennis is a busy surgeon. His two kids, introverted personality, and demanding work schedule provide all the excuses in the world for him to cut a check to the church, attend on Sundays, and consider his service to the church complete. But Dennis recognizes God's call on his life to be an integral part of the church family. This is why he opens up his home regularly to lead a community group and shares his life with other men so that he might disciple and counsel them faithfully (even if he might not use those words).

Abby recently graduated high school and is settling into her new life as a college student. Her friends have all kinds of different issues, from struggles with their parents, to academic pressure, to the many different social temptations that come with newfound freedom. Abby's experiencing some of these same struggles too, but even in the midst of her own mess it is obvious that God wants to use her in the lives of her friends and classmates. So she seeks to regularly be the listening ear and trusted confidant her friends need, and to do what she can to point them to the life-giving truth of the gospel.

What about you? What life stage are you in? What is your role? What story could be written about you? Wherever you are, God has laid before you an opportunity. More accurately, he has laid before you a responsibility. Whether you are a brand-new Christian or have been a Christian for half a century; whether you're the pastor of a small church in the city, a large church in the country, or a mega-church in the suburbs; whether you're a farmer, civil engineer, librarian, or a health inspector; whether you're a student or a professor: God has called you to speak the truth in love to those around you. You are an integral part of his plan to grow and mature the other Christians around you. You are called to minister in the midst of the mess. You are called to gospel care.

ENDNOTES

1. Paul Tripp, *Instruments in the Redeemer's Hands*, xi.
2. Jerry Bridges, *Crisis in Caring*, 9.
3. Colin Marshall and Tony Payne, *The Trellis and the Vine*.

CHAPTER 2

THE GOAL AND THE GOSPEL

George and Naomi sat down in our family room with one goal in mind: they wanted me to fix their marriage. Their marriage had become a pretty significant mess and they didn't know what to do about it. George wasn't a Christian and had resisted the idea of talking to anyone about their marriage. He figured that their marriage was their business and didn't see the need to talk about it with anyone else. However, Naomi had finally had enough. She couldn't keep living the way they were living and insisted that the two of them meet with somebody, *anybody*, and the lucky "somebody" was me. When they sat down, it was obvious that I was going to need to earn George's trust. He wasn't ready to hear anything from anyone, especially a pastor, but he was at least willing to be there. On the face of it, it seemed obvious that he was the one who was going to require the most engagement, but things aren't always what they seem.

We spent the majority of our first few times together getting to know one another. I asked a lot of questions and shared a bit about some of the similar struggles I'd had in my own marriage. The guidance I gave them at first wasn't anything special, but just some commonsense relational tips. I encouraged them to set aside time each day to talk intentionally with one another. I had them identify some specific ways they could show their love for one another. And I had them begin to share a calendar in order to minimize their miscommunications in scheduling.

After a couple weeks of applying these simple tasks, their relationship began to change. Their fights weren't as frequent and their schedules weren't as chaotic. I could see that I was earning George's trust. We were making progress toward their goal and they were enjoying the results. It was becoming obvious, however, that it was time to convey to both George and Naomi that the problem with their marriage wasn't just that they didn't have the right solutions, but that they were also working toward the wrong goal.

I told George and Naomi how encouraged I was by the diminishing friction in their marriage, and how glad I was that the tips I had given them were helpful. But then I told them that if they actually wanted to fix what was most fundamentally wrong with their marriage, they were going to need more than tips. The truth was, the problems they were experiencing went far deeper than communication and scheduling. If they were truly going to address the root of their problems, we needed to talk about their hearts. When I finished explaining this to them, George looked at me for a second and, to my surprise, simply said, "OK. What's wrong with my heart?"

George's response startled me for a second. I'm not sure I had ever had someone who wasn't a Christian open the door so widely. So I proceeded to explain to him that God's goal for his marriage (and his life) wasn't just that he would have a good marriage, but that he would become more like Christ. And I explained that the only way that was possible was through faith in the grace and forgiveness offered through the gospel. George quickly latched on and wanted to know more. But, to my surprise, it was Naomi who turned out to be more hesitant.

Naomi liked the idea of George coming to faith and becoming more like Jesus, but she was resistant to the idea that God's goal in this trial was to make *her* more like Christ as well. It seemed clear to Naomi that the mess they were in was George's mess, not hers. After all, George was the non-Christian in the relationship, so the problem was with him, right? Slowly Naomi came to realize that it wasn't only George who had been aiming at the wrong target in their marriage; she had been, too. She had brought George to me looking for a biblical solution to their problems, but she soon realized that they didn't just need a more biblical solution; they needed a more biblical goal.

THE GOAL

Before we can identify the way forward in helping people in their messes, we need to first make sure that we have the right tools and that we're headed in the right direction. Things can get confusing in the midst of the mess. Stepping into someone's mess can be like having a huge wave crash right on top of you while swimming in the ocean. You can end up underwater, disoriented and confused, and not knowing which way is up (surfers call this being in the washing machine). But before you start swimming, searching for air, you need to make sure you're headed in the right direction. Otherwise, you may expend a ton of time and energy only to realize that you've gotten further from the air your body is desperately craving.

Almost every system to deal with people's messes caters to self-defined goals. Whether you want to be happier, calmer, more productive, more disciplined, or less stressed, there are countless self-help resources and professionals with the express purpose of helping you change in the exact ways you desire. We define our own messes, and so we also define our own goals of change.

However, if we are going to follow God's call to speak the truth in love to one another, we must first clarify what the goal of that love-filled truth is. More specifically, we must make sure that *our* goal is in line with *God's* goal. Thankfully, God has communicated his goal for our ministry clearly and repeatedly in Scripture.

God's will for our lives as Christians is no secret. His goal for us is not simply that we would have better marriages, be less anxious, be happier, or feel fulfilled (although those are all natural byproducts of his goal). God's goal for us is that we would become more like Christ. Having reconciled us to himself through Christ, God is in the process of transforming us more and more into his image. As Scripture communicates so clearly:

> *For this is the will of God, your sanctification . . .*
> *(1 Thess. 4:3)*

> *For we are his workmanship, created in Christ*
> *Jesus for good works, which God prepared*
> *beforehand, that we should walk in them.*
> *(Eph. 2:10)*

Consequently, God's goal for our ministry to one another must be to help one another become more like Christ too. There are all sorts of different goals we could pursue, but only helping one another grow closer to Christ and become more like him can accurately be described as "truthing in love."

When God's goal becomes our goal, we won't be encouraging others to pursue their own passions and desires. We won't be trying to help people identify and achieve their self-focused dreams. Instead, we will be reminding them of the truth, implications, and expectations of the gospel. We'll be reminding them that "those who belong to Christ Jesus have crucified the flesh with its passions and desires" (Gal. 5:24). We'll be reminding them what God has designed them for, and what he has promised to produce in them. His Spirit dwells in every Christian and naturally produces Christlikeness in the midst of every one of our messes: "But the fruit of the Spirit is love, joy, peace, patience, kindness, goodness, faithfulness, gentleness, self-control; against such things there is no law" (Gal. 5:22–23).

Interestingly, if you listen to the mess of any Christian's heart, the opposite of that struggle is inevitably described here in this list. This is what it means to say that Scripture truly is sufficient for all of life. The sanctifying work of the Spirit addresses every aspect of the mess we experience. But when we define our own goals, we find that, while they are similar, those goals simply don't go deep enough.

In the midst of marital strife we want to get our own way, but God wants to produce love, peace, and faithfulness. In the midst of depression we want happiness, but God wants to give us lasting joy. In the midst of anger we want to be able to stay calm, but God wants to produce true peace and gentleness. In the midst of overeating we want to lose a few pounds, but God wants us to develop true self-control in all areas of our lives.

God wants to go deeper. He is after our hearts. He wants us to be like him. This is what he created us for, and what he re-created us for. Our goal in personal ministry must be his goal. Many of us have seen that embarrassing moment when a young basketball player gets ahold of the ball, takes off on a fast break, and finishes with a perfect layup, only to quickly realize that he has gotten turned around and scored on his opponent's hoop. His intention was sincere, his effort was strenuous, and his execution flawless; the only problem was, he had his sights set on the wrong goal. The wrong goal changes everything, and this is never more true than when it comes to helping others in the midst of their messes. The goal of all biblical personal ministry is to help one another become more like Jesus.

This is why the messy people in our lives need more than just our attention; they need the gospel. Whether they've been a Christian for days (like George) or decades (like Naomi), there is no truth they need more than the gospel. We're going to cover the gospel more thoroughly in chapters 11 to 14, but let's just look briefly at why the gospel is so central to achieving God's goal for our ministry to one another.

THE GOSPEL

When we're aiming at our own goals, we tend to use our own means. Without an external authority, we default to using whatever it seems "works" best. This is how everything from a conversation with a friend to a session with a therapist to a psychiatric medication is evaluated. Did it "work"? Of course, what we mean by "work" is, "Did it help achieve the goal I have set for myself to be happier/less anxious/more productive etc.?" Unfortunately there is no conversation, no professional, and no pill that alone can make you more like Christ. If we are going to aim for a biblical goal, we need biblical means.

The chief provision God has made for our sanctification (the process of becoming more like Jesus) is the gospel. When I say "the gospel," what I mean is both the message of the gospel and the implications of the gospel. The message of the gospel, which is applied to us through faith in Christ, is summed up in 1 Peter 3:18: "For Christ also suffered once for sins, the righteous for the unrighteous, that he might bring us to God, being put to death in the flesh but made alive in the spirit."

However, being reconciled to God is not the only blessing that we receive through faith in Christ. The New Testament lists numerous implications of the gospel that are also given to us and ought to be considered part of the "good news" contained in "the gospel." In Christ we are also adopted (Eph. 1:4), born again (1 Peter 1:3), guarded (1 Peter 1:5), forgiven (1 John 2:12), made heirs (Rom. 8:17), set free (Rom. 8:2), and so much more!

If we are going to help others become more like Christ, we have to start by calling them back, again and again, to the truth of the gospel. We have to encourage their Spirit-empowered effort to be motivated by God's love and grace. As Elyse Fitzpatrick and Dennis Johnson put it so beautifully, "Sanctification is never advanced by self-focused grief or guilt. It is energized by joy and driven by love. . . . Only a remembrance of the gospel will free us from our habitual grief and guilt. Only the gospel can implant the joy and love in our hearts that will free, motivate, and inspire us."[1]

When we call one another back to the truth of the gospel, we throw fuel on each other's love for God. This love for God is then put into practice through the hard work of bringing our thoughts, emotions, and behaviors more and more into conformity with Christ. The entire New Testament is filled with reminders of the truth of the gospel preceding practical instructions (for example, Eph. 1–3 vs. 4–6; Rom. 1–11 vs. 12–16; Col. 1–2 vs. 3–4). Paul even provides a condensed version of this in his letter to Titus:

> But when the goodness and loving kindness
> of God our Savior appeared, he saved us, not
> because of works done by us in righteousness,
> but according to his own mercy, by the washing
> of regeneration and renewal of the Holy Spirit,
> whom he poured out on us richly through Jesus
> Christ our Savior, so that being justified by his
> grace we might become heirs according to the
> hope of eternal life. The saying is trustworthy,
> and I want you to insist on these things, so that
> those who have believed in God may be careful to
> devote themselves to good works. These things
> are excellent and profitable for people.
>
> (Titus 3:4–8)

Paul begins by renewing the reader's mind with gospel truth. God saved us. He didn't save us because of our own righteous works, but "according to his own mercy." He saved us through his own "goodness and loving kindness." He sent his Son to pay the penalty we deserve for our sin and invites us into his family through faith. What life-altering truth! It doesn't matter how long we've been Christians, we all need to be reminded of the gospel daily.

Notice, though, that Paul doesn't simply state the fact of the gospel, he also renews the reader's mind with gospel implications. As glorious as our salvation is, God has done so much more through the gospel than simply save us. In this passage, Paul reminds Titus that God also regenerates us and makes us alive. He renews us by the power of his Holy Spirit. That same Spirit is also poured out on us so that we might possess his power. He has justified us by the blood of Christ. And he has made us his children and therefore heirs of the entire universe. When we are reminded of these kinds of gospel implications, it changes everything (as we will look at more deeply in chapter 13).

But Paul's reminder of both the message and the implications of the gospel has a goal in mind. There's a reason he wants Titus to "insist" on these truths. The reason is: "so that those who have believed in God may be careful to devote themselves to good works." In addition to reminding others of gospel truth and gospel implications, we must also remind them of gospel expectations. God expects the gospel to change our lives in tangible ways (as we will look at more deeply in chapter 14). The natural byproduct of the gospel taking root and growing in our hearts is our lives becoming shaped into the image Christ. Therefore, if the goal of our ministry is to help one another become more like Christ, we must recognize the central role the gospel plays in that process.

THE SUFFICIENCY OF SCRIPTURE

If you've read this far, I'm assuming that you are—at least in some way—compelled by the authority of Scripture. Every point that has been made has been rooted in the authority of God as he has revealed himself in his Word. It is through Scripture that God calls us to speak the truth to one another (Eph. 4:15). It is through Scripture that God communicates to us the goal of our lives and ministries: becoming more like Christ (1 Thess. 4:3). It is through Scripture that God specifies what becoming more like Christ looks like (Gal. 5:22–24). It is through Scripture that

God delivers the message of the gospel that empowers this transformation (Titus 3:4–7).

I've found that most Christians struggle less with the authority of Scripture than they do with the sufficiency of Scripture. You may agree that Scripture is authoritative for everything it speaks about. But you may still be confused about what exactly it addresses and what it doesn't. There are excellent books that have shown how Scripture is sufficient for every struggle in life,[2] and countless resources on specific struggles that practically demonstrate Scripture's sufficiency.[3] But that is not my goal here. As you read *this* book, my hope is that you will become convinced of how completely sufficient Scripture is for showing us *how* to speak the truth in love to one another. Scripture teaches us, with beautiful comprehensiveness, how to be a friend, mentor, counselor, or discipler in the midst of one another's messes.

While that may all sound good, the problem is that many of us still feel like we don't know what to do. Whether it's Amy, Abe, Nancy, Brian, Jenni, Dennis, or Abby, a common theme runs through the lives of many of the people I see wanting to minister to those around them: they are convinced that they are called to speak the truth in love, they know a certain amount of biblical truth, they may even have read some Christian books or articles on related topics, but they still aren't sure what to actually *do*. Where do they start? What should they say? What should they *not* say? How should they use Scripture? When should they use Scripture? How do they apply the gospel? How do they go deeper than just surface-level change? Where do they turn when they feel in over their heads?

Thankfully, God has not left us on our own to answer these questions. Not only does Scripture sufficiently provide us with the goal of our ministry and the gospel to empower it, but it also provides us with the tools and guidance to get there. Scripture not only tells us that we are called to speak the truth in love, but *how* to speak it as well. In his Word, God not only gives us a calling, he also gives us a plan for fulfilling that calling. The rest of this book is dedicated to exploring and unpacking that plan.

THE PLAN

So how do we minister to one another? What's the plan? Throughout the New Testament, God gives us dozens of one-another commands that together define for us what the plan of personal ministry entails. We often view all of these one-anothers separately, but, when we put them together, they provide us with a holistic approach to personal ministry that towers over all other models in its usefulness, completeness, and beauty. No model for relationships (social or therapeutic) comes close to the description of Christian friendships and personal ministry we find in Scripture.

For the sake of this book, we are going to call these relationships of speaking the truth in love "gospel care." Gospel care is the art of loving another person in order to help them become more like Jesus. Or, more specifically:

> *Gospel care is the God-exalting, grace-saturated art of loving another person, through patiently knowing, sacrificially serving, truthfully speaking, and consistently applying the gospel in order to help them become more like Jesus.*

This, in summary, is the plan. This is how God desires to use us in the lives of others *to help them become more like Jesus.* And this plan breaks down into four summary categories that we are going to explore together.

Patiently knowing is a prerequisite to any word or action. There is no way you can minister effectively to someone without first knowing and understanding them deeply. We have all been the recipients of service and speech without knowledge, and it is discouraging at best and hurtful at worst. In order to lovingly minister to someone, we must first listen and seek to understand who they are and what they are experiencing, so that we can wisely determine what is most needed in any given moment.

Sacrificially serving is a part of gospel care that has gone out of vogue. When we think of personal ministry we tend to think of simply sitting and talking, yet the New Testament has no category for such one-dimensional ministry. The numerous service-oriented one-another commands in Scripture and our own personal experience both attest to the power of sacrificial service in ministering in the midst of the mess. We are called to be more than just the lips of Christ to those who are hurting and struggling; we are called to be his hands and feet as well.

Truthfully speaking is also an integral part of gospel care. While consistently applying the gospel is, undeniably, a spoken aspect of ministry, there are numerous other kinds of speech that are needed in relationships as well. As biblical friends, counselors, and disciplers, we must be hope-givers, affirmers, and confronters. We must speak truth into diverse situations in diverse ways.

Consistently applying the gospel (or "gospeling," as I like to call it) is the core of gospel care. While there is a great amount of good that can come from patiently knowing someone, sacrificially serving them, and speaking truth to them, the only hope for true transformation is to help them apply the gospel to whatever situation they find themselves in. We apply the gospel by helping them to see that their problems are worse than they realize, but that God's grace is also greater than they've ever imagined, and that in light of this grace they can live a life of repentance more radical than they ever thought possible.

But gospel care is more than simply knowing, serving, speaking, and "gospeling" others. In fact, each of these is actually an application of a deeper motivation that is central to all personal ministry. As the definition begins, "Gospel care is the God-exalting, grace-saturated art of *loving* another person." Gospel care is essentially a manifestation of love above everything else. In fact, without love, none of these activities could accurately be called biblical in any real sense.

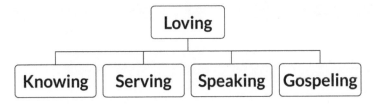

The love that motivates gospel care is a love that glorifies God as its source and motivation. The love expressed in gospel care points directly to the mercy of Christ and the magnitude of his grace. When you minister to someone, you do so as one messy person helping another messy person. As a fellow messy person, it is only natural that your love would be saturated by that same grace. The kingdom of God doesn't have any clean people available to minister to all the messy people who need help. Messy people like you and me are all God has at his disposal. And he loves to use messy people like us to befriend, counsel, and disciple other messy people.

So how do we do that? Well, as I've said, that's what we're going to explore together in the coming chapters, but in short, you befriend, counsel, and disciple other people simply by loving them. And you manifest that love by knowing them, serving them, speaking to them, and "gospeling" them. That's the plan.

But before we dig into the application of the plan, there's one more dynamic of gospel care we need to take a look at. You see, most of us, if we're honest, are pretty intimidated by other people's messes. We don't want some vague guidelines—we want a script. When we ask the question "How do we minister to one another?" we're looking less for general principles and more for specific verses, questions, or lines we can use. The problem is, as we'll see in the next chapter, gospel care is less of a science than an art. And to fulfill our calling to minister to those around us, we must embrace the artistic nature of our ministry.

So, are you ready? Maybe you've never tried your hand at this type of ministry before. Maybe you've been ministering to others for years, but you still feel like you have a lot of questions and insecurities. Maybe you've tried ministering to someone else a few times and feel way in over your head. No matter where you are, let me simply remind you that this is God's call on your life. He has placed you in the location you're in, with the relationships you have and the wisdom you possess, for a purpose. God wants to use you. The next step is simply to take a deeper look at his plan for how.

ENDNOTES

1. Elyse Fitzpatrick and Dennis Johnson, *Counsel from the Cross*, 118.
2. Examples include Tim Lane and Paul Tripp, *How People Change*; Elyse Fitzpatrick and Dennis Johnson, *Counsel from the Cross*; Heath Lambert and Stuart Scott, *Counseling the Hard Cases*.
3. I can't provide a complete list here, but, just to give you an idea, there are many biblical resources available that demonstrate Scripture's sufficiency in addressing issues like sexual struggles (Heath Lambert, *Finally Free*; Bobby Scott, *Secret Sex Wars*); addictions (Ed Welch, *Addictions: A Banquet in the Grave*); depression (Robert Somerville, *If I'm a Christian Why Am I Depressed?*); homosexuality (Jackie Hill Perry, *Gay Girl, Good God*; Caleb Kaltenbach, *Messy Grace*); domestic violence (Justin and Lindsey Holcomb, *Is It My Fault?*)—and the list could go on and on.

CHAPTER 3

THE UNSCRIPTED ART OF GOSPEL CARE

Ben and Lucy had some pretty typical struggles in their marriage. Lucy couldn't decide whether to keep her part-time job and the income it provided, or to stay at home with their young son. Her emotions swung back and forth between feelings of guilt for not being at home and feelings of weakness for not being able to handle her job. She would talk and talk about her feelings, but rarely end up any closer to a real decision. Ben is an engineer in both career and disposition. He couldn't understand why his wife was so emotional about every little thing in their lives, and all he wanted was for her to make a choice. By the time I sat down with them, he didn't even care which choice she made. He just wanted it to be done so they could move on.

As I sat in their family room one evening, their son having already gone to sleep, I noticed just how far the two of them had drifted apart. They sat on the same couch somehow having transformed from partners into adversaries. It seemed as though neither of them could step outside of their own perspective long enough to communicate clearly with one another, and even though this moment didn't have to be a crisis in their marriage, it had become one.

I've sat with countless couples in similar situations. But as I looked into the eyes of these two hurting people, I realized that I didn't have a textbook answer to give them. I didn't have five steps to a wonderful marriage or a handbook to clear communication. I didn't even have one surefire Bible verse to set them on the path to marital bliss.

It wasn't that my study of Scripture was insufficient (even though there's always more to learn). The fact was, I did have many different tools, resources, and passages of Scripture at my disposal. But even though I had seen situations like Ben and Lucy's before, I had never experienced *this* situation. The variables at work in Ben and Lucy's lives were far more numerous than simply their life stage or emotional/rational makeup. Their struggles couldn't be summarized in a quick sentence or by the identification of a personality type.

Ben had grown up a Christian, but Lucy came to faith later in college. Ben grew up with a strong working mother in the Midwest. Lucy grew up with a difficult and troubled mother in the Southeast. Ben and Lucy love each other dearly, but there is much that they do not share in common, including economic background, familial stability, and ethnicity. These variables, and so many more, were impacting their communication, their expectations, and even the process by which they made decisions. It was for this reason that, as I sat with them that first night praying for wisdom, I realized that in all my years of counseling and discipling I had never faced a situation quite like the one they were experiencing. And what's more, that is always the case.

You see, gospel care is not a science. A relationship is not a controlled and regulated situation where you can expect the same outcome every time you introduce the same stimulus. Relationships are messy. Each "couple with communication problems" does not require the same passage of Scripture, practical tips, or book to read. Gospel care is an art. It is creative in nature and constantly in flux, always in need of contextualization in an ever-changing world full of variables.

Good science controls for variables so they don't interfere with the results of an experiment. But good art, instead of trying to get rid of variables, takes as many variables into consideration as possible and utilizes them for the power and relevance of the art form. This is especially true of improvisational art forms like jazz.

GOSPEL CARE AS JAZZ

Gospel care is a lot like jazz.[1] To start with, both jazz and gospel care are difficult to define. Even the definition I provided in the previous chapter can't perfectly summarize all that personal ministry entails. No definition can. Similarly, jazz critics have historically had great difficulty defining the genre. As Louis Armstrong put it, "If you have to ask what it is, you'll never know."

Nevertheless, through the years there have been numerous attempts to summarize jazz that have proven helpful, especially for those of us who didn't grow up listening to it. A simple definition of jazz would claim that it always includes two key elements: swing and improvisation. Swing speaks to the feel and rhythm of the music. As Duke Ellington famously sang, "It don't mean a thing if it ain't got that swing."

Improvisation, on the other hand, speaks to the individual creativity that is jazz's hallmark. While the underlying melody plays, the jazz musician is given an opportunity to improvise and make up a tune on the spot in order to contribute to the "musical event." Although it is built upon the foundation of the musician's skill, her previous experience, the history of the art form, and the tenor of the song, the exact notes the jazz soloist plays are not pre-scripted. Neither is the rhythm, tone, or timbre with which those notes are played. Jazz is unscripted.

Gospel care is improvisational in the same way. Your ministry to a friend may be built upon the foundation of your biblical knowledge, wisdom, life experience, ministry experience, and knowledge of the person and situation. But the words you choose to speak and the actions you choose to take are not predetermined. They are improvised in the context of the relationship. There is no script for gospel care.

MOVING BEYOND THE SCRIPT

Now, emphasizing the improvisational nature of personal ministry may make you feel a little uneasy. The truth is that most of us don't want to improvise. When life gets messy, we begin scrambling around looking for a script, or searching for someone (or something) to tell us exactly what to say and do, especially when we feel like we're in over our heads.

And that's the problem, isn't it? We don't struggle with improvisation in situations where we feel comfortable. But as soon as we are outside of our comfort zone, we begin searching frantically for a script. That's why the most common question I get as a pastor is, "What should I say to someone in this situation?" We don't like the responsibility of having to improvise. I mean, what if we say the wrong thing? We just want the "right answer."

This type of nervousness ought to be expected. It's the normal reaction of anyone learning an improvisational art form. But that doesn't mean that it's without consequences. The fact is, whenever improvisational artists search for a script, they usually end up performing worse (not better) than if they had simply practiced their craft and then taken a stab on their own. R. Keith Sawyer, an expert on creativity and professor at the University of North Carolina, explains this dynamic in his book *Group Creativity*:

> *When faced with the uncertainty of improvisation, beginners have a tendency to want to establish structure and script as quickly as possible. This can lead them to try to guess how the other actors will respond to the utterance they are considering, and thus to already be thinking ahead to their own next turn. Not only does this lead to too much conscious planning and a delay before speaking: it also prevents the beginner from listening closely to the partner's response and responding to it.*[2]

The beginning jazz student runs into all sorts of problems when he looks for a script. He ends up overthinking his choices, allowing his mind to jump two or three decisions ahead, and making assumptions that may or may not be accurate. He is unnatural and delayed in his responses because they are so overcooked. And, worst of all, his search for a script has crippled his ability to listen, to *really listen*, to the other participants in the musical conversation.

We'll explore the importance of listening in chapter 5, but let me just say this for now: gospel care is unmoored at best and damaging at worst when it is not informed by careful, attentive listening. Listening allows us to determine which of the numerous passages of Scripture, resources, actions, or sentiments at our disposal are appropriate for the moment. And while ministering without a script doesn't hamper your ability to listen, constantly searching for one inevitably does.

BOUNDARIED IMPROVISATION

Having established that we are called to move beyond the script, you may now be asking, "But how far?" Shouldn't there be some sort of guideline or limits to our improvisation? Again, I think jazz provides us with a helpful analogy. Jazz is not simple spontaneous self-expression. The jazz musician's musical choices "must always play notes that fulfill the requirements of the context."[3] Again, Sawyer is helpful: "Improv does not mean 'anything goes.' In jazz, each musician and each group must balance two competing tendencies: the expectation of creativity and inspiration, and the need to maintain coherence with both the tradition and the group."[4]

In jazz, the musician must maintain coherence with the tradition and group. In gospel care, we must maintain coherence with the Word of God. The truth of Scripture provides the boundaries beyond which our improvisation cannot stray. The fact that Scripture is sufficient means that it speaks directly and powerfully to every single issue we face. As Paul reminded Timothy, this kind of personal ministry to one another is specifically what Scripture is "profitable for": "All Scripture is breathed out by God and profitable for teaching, for reproof, for correction, and for training in righteousness, that the man of God may be complete, equipped for every good work"(2 Tim. 3:16–17).

But, even more than this, the truth of Scripture also provides the focal point of our improvisation; it provides the melody that the improvisation serves and returns to. In jazz there is always an underlying melody that is the context for any improvisation. It supplies the foundational key, tempo, and feel that the improvisation is meant to reflect and compliment. As we will see in the next chapter, the melody for gospel care is the tune of Spirit-empowered love: "For this is the message that you have heard from the beginning, that we should love one another" (1 John 3:11).

Without boundaries, gospel care is unmoored. Without boundaries, we tend to simply share tips, suggestions, or opinions, not considering whether they are wise, helpful, or even true. Without improvisation, gospel care is impractical. Without improvisation, we try to follow some artificial script by regurgitating specific Bible verses or reciting overused Christian platitudes. Boundaries direct our words and shape our actions. Improvisation allows us to contextualize those words and actions to the needs of any given moment.

LEARNING THE ART

So, if gospel care is an artistic act of improvisation, how do we learn to do it? If there's no script to memorize, how do we grow and become better? Is the gift of personal ministry just something that some people have and other people don't? Of course not. As we saw in the first chapter, gospel care is something that every Christian is called to. But what does being trained and equipped in an art actually entail?

While jazz musicians rely heavily on improvisation, they still must learn musical skill and theory. To improvise well, you need to know music *better* than if you were just playing pre-scripted notes. Improvising well requires practicing the basics as well as experimenting with different riffs to discover what works and what doesn't. In fact, once they've found something that works, many jazz musicians will play a certain lick over and over until they own it and know that it will be easily available when the right moment comes in a song.

In the same way, the fact that gospel care is improvisational in nature ought to make us *more* committed to becoming equipped with biblical truth, not less. We must be avid students of God's Word, and collectors of practical wisdom and insight. We must be diligent to steep our hearts and minds in a biblical worldview if we are going to offer truth in love to the various people who come across our paths. In addition to simply spending time reading our Bibles, this may take the form of reading books or articles on specific issues or attending classes on discipleship or biblical counseling. We must also practice speaking truth to error and hope to despair in our own lives if we are ever going to be able to play those riffs for others.

Additionally, while practicing the basics is of the utmost importance, the greatest way to learn and grow as an improvisational musician is simply to play with more experienced people. As Stan Getz is believed to have said, "You can read all the textbooks and listen to all the records, but you *have* to play with musicians that are better than you."

This is why growing in our ability to provide gospel care must not be limited to taking a class, reading a book, or studying the Bible. It must also include coming alongside others who are wiser and more experienced than we are. One great way to start is to simply tag along with a fellow Christian as he or she talks with a brother or sister about life and God. Or you could just stop and listen the next time someone in your small group is speaking truth to a friend over dinner. Paul assumed this kind of intimate observation when he reminded the Philippians to emulate what they had "seen" in him: "What you have learned and received and heard *and seen in me*—practice these things, and the God of peace will be with you" (Phil. 4:9).[5]

My friend Dave is a jazz musician and loves playing music more than anyone I know. One afternoon, he described to me the arc of his musicianship, and it made me realize just how similar it is to the process of learning to minister to others. When Dave began playing the bass, he knew he was bad. He didn't even know how to hold the instrument, and everything he tried was hard (maybe that's how you feel about gospel care). But, as he practiced, things became more natural. He began to get the sense that he understood both how to play and what to play when. He then improved to a point where he had gained a lot of confidence and, while he knew he wasn't "great," he (in his words) "didn't suck anymore."

Eventually Dave became good. Really good. He relished his ability and talent, and considered himself "a great musician." Dave describes this point in his musicianship as "murderous." The pride and hubris he experienced were lethal to his continued growth and development.

And then came a wake-up call. But Dave's pride wasn't crushed by some confrontation with another epic bassist. He didn't experience a lightning bolt from heaven. Subtly, as he played with other musicians, he began to see areas where he still had a lot of room to grow. He began to realize that there is no ceiling on growth and development as a musician. There's actually more to be developed and discovered than you could ever uncover in a lifetime. As Dizzy Gillespie once said, "It's taken me all my life to learn what not to play."[6] It was then that Dave realized that, even with all of his talent and hard work, he was much closer to that fifteen-year-old with a brand-new bass than he had wanted to admit. In fact, he still had *a lot* to learn.

That's true about you and me, too. No matter how long we've been ministering to others, no matter how much or how little training we've received, we are much closer to that novice Christian we began as than we would ever care to admit. We're all in the same boat together, still learning and growing. But just because we have room to grow doesn't mean God doesn't want to use us *as* we grow. Unlike Dave, however, we need something more than just training in order to minister effectively in the midst of the mess. Hard work and diligent practice alone can't fully prepare us for what God has called us to. We need something supernatural.

The Spiritual Dynamic

In our own strength and abilities, all the training and equipping in the world can't cause us to minister to one another effectively. If the goal of our ministry is to facilitate gospel transformation, we need spiritual empowerment.

This is one of the points at which the jazz analogy falls apart. Many jazz musicians will talk about the "spiritual dynamic" of music when the melody and the beat carry you along and you begin to make decisions without even thinking about it. And music does have powerful access to the depths of our souls. But the "spiritual dynamic" of music is not even comparable to the empowerment that comes for the Christian who has the Spirit of God dwelling in their heart. The art of gospel care is carried along at every moment by the Spirit of God in both you and (if he or she is a Christian) the person you are ministering to.

The indwelling of the Spirit impacts gospel care in numerous ways, and space doesn't allow for mentioning all of them here. But, just to get a taste of the centrality of the Spirit's work in gospel care, let's look at three significant ways the Spirit empowers you to minister effectively to others.

First, the Spirit teaches us and reminds us of truth. Everything we know and have to offer to others is implanted in our hearts and brought to our minds by the Spirit. Everything we've gleaned from the pages of Scripture, we have come to understand through the Spirit enlightening our minds. When preparing to leave his disciples, Jesus assured them, "But the Helper, the Holy Spirit, whom the Father will send in my name, he will teach you all things and bring to your remembrance all that I have said to you" (John 14:26).

Ministering improvisationally can be a scary thing. You may feel like you wouldn't know what to say or do. But we have a supernatural reason for confidence. Not only does the Spirit take what we have learned and teach it to the depths of our hearts, but he also brings what we've learned to our remembrance at just the right time.

Second, it is the Spirit who grants us the wisdom we so desperately need to care lovingly for others. Ministering to another person in the midst of the complexity of their mess requires an incredible amount of wisdom and discernment. Thankfully, God not only teaches us *about* wisdom (Proverbs, Ecclesiastes, etc.), but he also promises that if we come to him seeking wisdom, he will give it to us: "If any of you lacks wisdom, let him ask God, who gives generously to all without reproach, and it will be given him" (James 1:5). What an incredible promise! If you ask for wisdom, "it will be given" to you. Now that's an unambiguous biblical promise that you can take to the bank. And the avenue for us to receive this wisdom is through the indwelling Spirit of God.

Third, and most encouragingly, the one who is ultimately responsible for bringing about the transformation that is the goal of gospel care is *not* you. It's the Spirit of God working in the person you are ministering to. As we talked about in the last chapter, the goal of gospel care is to bring about Christlikeness. The goal, again, is not simply to help someone become more "mature" or even to see his or her problematic emotional symptoms go away. The goal is that he or she would increase in joy and self-control, peace and kindness. And Scripture tells us quite explicitly that these are not the fruit of good personal ministry or even of wise discipleship. These are fruit of the Spirit: "But the fruit of the Spirit is love, joy, peace, patience, kindness, goodness, faithfulness, gentleness, self-control; against such things there is no law. And those who belong to Christ Jesus have crucified the flesh with its passions and desires. If we live by the Spirit, let us also keep in step with the Spirit" (Gal. 5:22–25). The Spirit of God, working in a person's heart, is the one who brings about the transformation that is the ultimate goal of gospel care.

When we look at all of the ways the Spirit of God is working, we can be encouraged that we are not left alone or helpless. In fact, we are called to improvisational personal ministry while being empowered and guided by the very Spirit who spoke through the prophets and raised Christ from the dead. This should lead us to expect *more* than if we were following a script. It's not just that he's going to give us the right words, it's that we're a part of something bigger than ourselves—we're being guided and carried along by God himself. There is a song being played that we're a part of, but we don't set the tempo or the key. We're just participants, contributors, and enjoyers of *his* song.

Now we can improvise with confidence, not because we are so experienced, talented, or knowledgeable, but because the Spirit of God actually lives inside us and is empowering us every step of the way. As Francis Chan once wrote, "I don't want my life to be explainable without the Holy Spirit. I want people to look at my life and know that I couldn't be doing this by my own power. I want to live in such a way that I am desperate for him to come through."[7] I don't want my ministry to others to be explainable without the Holy Spirit, either. All of our improvisation should be desperately dependent upon the Spirit of God, and unexplainable without his active presence. For gospel care to have any lasting impact, he *has* to come through.

CATCHING THE MELODY

As I think back to that moment in Ben and Lucy's apartment, I can see how active the Spirit of God was in our conversation that evening and the many evenings afterward. For all of its normalcy, I still had never encountered a situation exactly like the one they were going through. But, as God wove my imperfect words and actions together, his Spirit used them to transform both of their hearts, which produced real change in their marriage. They began to understand one another better, serve one another more sacrificially, and communicate more clearly than they ever had before.

I like to look back and think of those conversations as a song. It was a song that I got to play a part in, and one that I'd heard before. But the notes I played that night were new; they were unique, because the people and the moment were unique. We experienced a God-event that night, much like the God-events that take place countless times every day, but also completely unlike any other one.

The greatest commonality between that night and all of the other moments of ministry I've experienced is the melody that forms the foundation of the song. It's the melody of love. It was first established (the rhythm and notes being set) by God's love through Christ. So, if we are to join in the song and contribute beautifully through our Spirit-led improvisation, we must first make sure that we grasp the melody and know intimately the song that was first played for us.

ENDNOTES

1. I am indebted to David "Gunner" Gundersen who introduced this specific analogy to me over a conversation about the artistic nature of ministry.
2. R. Keith Sawyer, *Group Creativity*, 56.
3. *The Cambridge Companion to Jazz*, 134.
4. Sawyer, *Group Creativity*, 51.
5. All emphasis in Scripture quotes has been added.
6. Larry Kemo, *Early Jazz Trumpet Legends*, xii
7. Francis Chan, *Forgotten God*, 142.

CHAPTER 4

THE MELODY OF LOVE

O ur relationship began on the patio of a fast-food restaurant. Jamal was a student at a local art college, and I was the pastor of a new church plant in the area. A mutual friend had met Jamal at a wedding and suggested we connect. Jamal's previous experience with pastors was not great. He had been misled, lied to, and manipulated by those he looked up to both spiritually and emotionally. And now he was sitting on the corner of a busy LA street, eating a burrito and sipping a Diet Coke with someone he had just met and didn't know if he could trust.

It has been ten years since that moment we met. And over that decade Jamal has become one of my closest confidants and dearest friends. But sitting there dipping my chip into a tiny little plastic cup of salsa, I could never have imagined all the different forms our relationship would take, nor how powerfully God wanted to use Jamal and me in each other's lives.

My relationship with Jamal has taken a number of different shapes over the years. For a while it took the form of what I would have called discipleship. For a significant amount of time it took the form of in-depth counseling as he battled both habitual sin and deep hurt from the neglect and manipulation of his father. During one period it took the form of housemates when he moved in with me, my wife, and our newborn baby.

At other points in our relationship the dynamic could probably best be described as mentoring, and eventually it developed into both shepherding and deep friendship. Throughout all of these different seasons of relationship, Jamal has grown incredibly in his relationship with Christ. And so have I. At times, the Lord has used my words or actions to communicate truth and love in a way that has shaped Jamal's view of God and drawn him into a deeper relationship with him. At other times, however, my poorly chosen words or self-centered actions have caused Jamal more pain or confusion, and I have had to seek Jamal's forgiveness and grace.

There have been so many different moments I have experienced with Jamal, and so many different situations we have found ourselves in. Over the years I have listened and talked, confronted and affirmed, been strong and been gentle, prayed and jumped into action. We've met in coffee shops, living rooms, parked cars, restaurants, church offices, parks, and numerous other places.

So, what do you call this kind of gospel care? How do you describe a multifaceted relationship that results in both of you becoming more like Christ? Scripture gives us one summary term for this kind of ministry and relationship: love.

THE GREATEST COMMANDMENT

All personal ministry can be summed up in four simple words: Love God, love people. Love is the melody of gospel care. In fact, it's the melody of the entire Christian life. *Everything* you and I are called to is essentially an application of our love for God and our love for people. As I've mentioned, this is not just the job description of a pastor or the assignment of a missionary; it is the calling of every Christian. We learn this from Jesus' own mouth:

> *And one of them, a lawyer, asked him a*
> *question to test him. "Teacher, which is the*
> *great commandment in the Law?" And he*
> *said to him, "You shall love the Lord your God*
> *with all your heart and with all your soul and*
> *with all your mind. This is the great and first*
> *commandment. And a second is like it: You*
> *shall love your neighbor as yourself. On these*
> *two commandments depend all the Law and*
> *the Prophets."*
>
> *(Matt. 22:35–40)*

We were created to love and worship God. He is our Creator, our Savior, our Father, our Lord, our Redeemer, our Judge, our Beloved, and our God. The love that we have for him is only in response to the unimaginable love he has for us. When I reflect on God's love, I often remember the words of the old hymn, "The Love of God":

> *Could we with ink the ocean fill,*
> *And were the skies of parchment made,*
> *Were every stalk on earth a quill,*
> *And every man a scribe by trade;*
> *To write the love of God above*
> *Would drain the ocean dry;*
> *Nor could the scroll contain the whole,*
> *Though stretched from sky to sky.*[1]

This is the love that was demonstrated in the most radical way through God sending his Son to pay the penalty you and I deserve for our rebellion. As we take time to consider what God has done for us through Christ, we can begin to get a sense of just how immense his love is. And the more we understand of Christ's love, the more we come to understand love itself. For it's through Christ that God defines for us what love is: "In this is love, not that we have loved God but that he loved us and sent his Son to be the propitiation for our sins" (1 John 4:10).

Having received such love, it is only natural that we would love him in return. Scripture tells us that our love for God can take many different forms. We love God through prayer, obedience, singing, and sacrifice, but most fundamentally our love for God takes the form of loving others: "Beloved, if God so loved us, we also ought to love one another. No one has ever seen God; if we love one another, God abides in us and his love is perfected in us" (1 John 4:11-12).

This is why loving God and loving others go hand in hand. God created us to worship him and to love him. And one of the key ways we show our love for him is by humbly and sacrificially loving others. Loving others is not just a part of gospel care—it *is* gospel care. As I mentioned at the end of the last chapter, love is the key foundational component of all personal ministry. Love is the melody of gospel care.

LOVE SUMMARIZES

Loving others, while exciting in theory, isn't simple. In fact, one of the greatest hurdles to many of us ministering the Word to others is the apparent complexity of what's involved. First of all, the Bible is a complex book. It's really long. And it's not the simplest book to read, either. It's made up of all sorts of different types of literature written during different centuries. And it's not even organized by topic! Trying to figure out where to turn in this gigantic book can be overwhelming.

Not only is Scripture complex, but the people you are trying to minister to are incredibly complex as well. They have unique experiences and knowledge that you don't fully know or understand. Their emotions or actions will often defy simple explanation. Regardless of how hard our world tries to categorize people and their problems into nice, neat diagnoses, most people don't fit neatly into any one box. Their struggles are unique, their experiences are unique, and their reactions are unique.

And it's into this mess that we are called to take the overwhelmingly complex content of Scripture and apply it to the overwhelmingly complex people in front of us. Talk about a mess! It's no wonder that so many of us shy away from our calling to befriend, counsel, or disciple one another. We feel inadequate.

Thankfully, while both people and the Word of God are more complex than the most learned psychologist or biblical scholar will ever fully comprehend, God is not confused by this complexity. He created it. As the one who knows each one of us completely, he summarizes all that we are to know and do in ways that are simple enough for even the newest Christian to understand. This is why he summarizes all gospel care into this one simple instruction: love.

> *Owe no one anything, except to love each other, for the one who loves another has fulfilled the law. For the commandments, "You shall not commit adultery, You shall not murder, You shall not steal, You shall not covet," and any other commandment, are summed up in this word:*

"You shall love your neighbor as yourself." Love does no wrong to a neighbor; therefore love is the fulfilling of the law.

(Rom. 13:8–10)

LOVE UNIFIES

I'm a little ashamed to admit it, but after five years of mowing my own lawn (or mowing my own weeds, as the case may be), I finally broke down and asked the guy who mows all of my neighbors' lawns to add me to his routine. The first week he started, however, something strange happened. He came by and trimmed a few of our bushes, and then my wife, Lara, didn't see him for an entire hour. Then he came back and mowed the lawn, but again disappeared. Finally, another hour later, he came back and blew all of the yard trimmings off the sidewalk and patio. Lara called me, giggling about what had just happened and bewildered by the unorthodox schedule our new gardener seemed to keep.

We laughed a bit about how other parts of life would look if we performed our tasks the way our gardener seemed to function, but then it dawned on me: maybe there was some sort of larger plan or strategy that actually made sense of this odd progression. And, of course, there was. My gardener has so many houses on the same street that he finds it most efficient to trim everyone's bushes, then mow everyone's lawn, and then blow the trimmings off everyone's sidewalks. There was a greater purpose that brought unity to the seemingly arbitrary timing of my gardener's tasks.

Similarly, love not only summarizes all the different words and actions involved in gospel care, but it unifies them as well. One day we may be rebuking someone, and the next we may be encouraging them. We may forgive a person one day, and then ask them for forgiveness the next. We may cry or laugh, talk or be silent, walk or sit. But what brings unity to all of these diverse relational interactions is love. Paul teaches as much in his letter to the Colossians:

Put on then, as God's chosen ones, holy and beloved, compassionate hearts, kindness,

humility, meekness, and patience, bearing with
one another and, if one has a complaint against
another, forgiving each other; as the Lord has
forgiven you, so you also must forgive. And above
all these put on love, which binds everything
together in perfect harmony.

(Col. 3:12–14)

Love brings coherence to all the words we speak and actions we take in gospel care. Love makes discipleship real and applicable as it causes us to change and adapt according to what is needed and what will be most helpful. Love makes a counseling relationship explode with vitality because of its diverse and timely responses. Love makes mentoring more than a one-way street; it forms a bond and a mutual dynamic that cause both the mentor and the mentee to become more like Christ. Love provides the foundation and unity for everything we hope to call gospel care.

WHAT IS LOVE?

But what is love? One time, after completing an hour-long seminar on this topic, I was approached by a kind but concerned-looking man. He expressed his thankfulness for the content, but had just one lingering question: What *is* love? In that moment, standing with this older gentleman, I muttered some sort of answer that I can only hope was semi-coherent, but all I can remember is that inside I was panicking. I had just spent an entire hour talking about the importance of love, and I wasn't even sure I could provide a clear, succinct definition of what love actually *is*.

Well, the truth is, I'm not sure I'm much closer to providing that clear, succinct definition today than I was then. The only difference is that I'm not panicked about it anymore. There's a reason why philosophers, musicians, theologians, and poets have tirelessly tried to help us understand love without one clear definition reigning supreme. It's because there's a mystery to love. Love defies simple definition.

This is why we find descriptions and explanations of love all over the pages of Scripture. God teaches us what love is by describing it, illustrating it, and (most practically) modeling it. We know what love is because of his love for us. Of course, the few pages dedicated to love in this book can't come anywhere near to communicating a comprehensive answer to the question "What is love?" But we can at least take a couple of steps toward a better understanding of love by looking at three different ways love manifests itself. Specifically, that love for others is demonstrated in our thoughts, our emotions, and our actions.

LOVE IN THOUGHTS

First, *love manifests itself in our thoughts.* Loving someone means thinking of him or her in a certain way. It means, in fact, thinking of them as more significant than ourselves.

> *Do nothing from selfish ambition or conceit, but*
> *in humility count others more significant than*
> *yourselves. Let each of you look not only to his own*
> *interests, but also to the interests of others. Have*
> *this mind among yourselves, which is yours in Christ*
> *Jesus, who, though he was in the form of God, did*
> *not count equality with God a thing to be grasped,*
> *but emptied himself, by taking the form of a servant,*
> *being born in the likeness of men. And being found*
> *in human form, he humbled himself by becoming*
> *obedient to the point of death, even death on a cross.*
> *(Phil. 2:3–8)*

Loving others the way Christ does means thinking of others the way Christ did. The mind of Christ has one overwhelming characteristic: humility. I like the way that the New American Standard Bible phrases it: "regard one another as more important than yourselves" (Phil. 2:3). We aren't only called to act as if others are more important than us, we're called to actually think it. Love goes far beyond traditional boundaries in relationships. The truth is, we may be comfortable with *acting* humble or *acting* as if others are more important than we are, but we cringe at the thought of actually thinking of them as more important. We cringe at the thought of actually *being* humble.

We have all been trained and conditioned to look out for ourselves first, and to think of ourselves as the most significant, most important, or most special. But consider, just for a moment, the example that Christ set for us. Although he had existed from eternity past in the form of God, he loved us so much that he humbled himself by confining himself to an earthly body. God was born. Not only was he born, but he lived an earthly life of hunger, discomfort, temptation, and pain. And then he humbled himself to the point of a physically excruciating death and received the wrath of God that you and I deserve for our sin.

You have probably heard people talk about boundaries and having appropriate limits in relationships. Of course it is important to acknowledge our finiteness and confess that we do not have the capacity to be everything a person needs (we don't even have the capacity to be *most* of what they need). However, the motivations of self-preservation and personal comfort simply cannot be found in the example of Jesus. To love like Jesus loves means choosing to think like Jesus thought: in a consistently and sacrificially others-focused way.

LOVE IN EMOTIONS

However, love is more than just thinking differently about someone; *love also manifests itself in our emotions.* The emotional side of love has gotten a bad rap in the church in recent years. In light of the sentimental version of love promoted in popular culture, many in the church have sought to clarify that love is about more than how we feel. In fact, the church has thankfully demonstrated the misleading nature of *many* of our emotions. Feeling worthless doesn't mean that I am worthless. Feeling like God is distant doesn't mean that he is far off. And not feeling like loving someone doesn't give you license to be self-centered. However, Scripture and our personal experiences both consistently demonstrate that while love is much more than an emotion, it is not less. Love *does* have a powerfully emotional component.

You see, the problem is not that love involves our emotions, or even that love involves self-satisfying joy. The problem comes when we use "love" to seek our own self-centered joy. This, in fact, is not love of others at all, but really just a form of self-love. John Piper explains this in his classic book *Desiring God*:

*Love does not seek its own private, limited joy, but
instead seeks its own joy in the good—the salvation and
edification—of others. In this way we begin to love the way
God loves. He loves because he delights to love. He does not
seek to hide from himself the reward of love lest his act be
ruined by the anticipated joy that comes from it.*[2]

For God, the reward of love is the joy that comes from the impact
of love on the hearts of its recipients. Love seeks a shared joy.
Love rejoices with those who rejoice. Love weeps with those who
weep. And love rejoices in the comfort and bond produced by
weeping with those who weep.

Probably the most famous passage on love in all of Scripture
is 1 Corinthians 13. But while this passage is used in many
wedding ceremonies, its original context is not specifically in
reference to romantic love but rather brotherly love, the love of
gospel care. It comes right in the middle of a section dedicated
to how we serve, love, and care for one another in the body of
Christ. And it's in the context of this one-another ministry that
we get this poetic description:

> *Love is patient and kind; love does not envy or
> boast; it is not arrogant or rude. It does not insist
> on its own way; it is not irritable or resentful;
> it does not rejoice at wrongdoing, but rejoices
> with the truth. Love bears all things, believes all
> things, hopes all things, endures all things.*
>
> *(1 Cor. 13:4–7)*

Again, Piper is helpful here:

*The very definition of love in 1 Corinthians refutes [a]
narrow conception of love. For example, Paul says love
is not jealous and not easily provoked, and that it rejoices
in the truth and hopes all things (13:4–7). All these are
feelings! If you feel certain things such as unholy jealousy
and irritation, you are not loving. And if you do not feel
certain things such as joy in the truth and hope, you are not
loving. In other words, YES, love is more than feelings; but,
NO, love is not less than feelings.*[3]

Love, by its very nature, engages our emotions. Duty-compelled "selfless" thoughts are not reflective of the love of Christ. Christ has loved us with a passionate and emotionally engaged love, and he calls us to love others in this same way. Loving others the way Christ loves means feeling about others the way Christ feels. God calls us to actually *care* about other people, to be engaged in their lives and to *feel* alongside them. Reflecting the gospel means to emotionally *care*. This is a far cry from the typical protectionist ideal of a friend with "healthy boundaries." And it's a far cry from the typical therapeutic ideal of a detached and objective counselor who "doesn't get too involved." But, after all, our God is not a typical god.

Love in Actions

In addition to being manifest in our *thoughts* and our *emotions*, *love is also always manifested concretely in our actions*. Christ's love for us did not stop short of being put into action, and our love shouldn't either. Love is neither authentic nor complete until it demonstrates itself in tangible ways. Love is relational in nature, and the only way the thoughts and emotions we have talked about can be relational is for them to be put into practice through others-focused, joy-inducing actions.

The New Testament is full of instructions that help us to understand what love-in-action looks like. In fact, there are approximately forty-two different "one-another" commands, not to mention the numerous examples in the lives of Jesus, Peter, Paul, and others. These one-anothers form the instruction manual for what it means to provide gospel care.

How does God want us to minister to those around us? He wants us to love. So, all forms of ministry, whatever we call them, will necessarily involve the one-anothers that are all manifestations of that love.

As true as that is, if you were to look at a list of the biblical one-anothers, chances are you'd just get overwhelmed. After all, loving involves outdoing one another in showing honor, bearing with one another, exhorting one another, showing hospitality to one another, seeking to do good to one another, confessing to one another, encouraging one another, building one another up, admonishing one another, and a whole bunch more! How are you supposed to keep them all straight, let alone live genuinely with another person, with all of these different commands flying around in your head?

This reminds me of one of my co-pastor Brian's favorite illustrations. Trying to keep all of the biblical one-anothers straight is kind of like trying to learn a golf swing. A golf swing is a complicated action. Almost all of your body is in motion, and whatever mistakes you make are magnified by the fact that you're trying to hit a tiny ball with a tiny head on the end of a long, skinny stick. As a result, there are lots of different tips that you need to keep in mind. Far too many well-meaning parents have stood behind their children spouting off a well-rehearsed litany of: keep your back straight, don't bend your elbow, *do* bend your knees, keep your head down, draw the club back not up, don't hold the club too firm, don't let it slip, don't lift your front foot, etc. This results in the child (of any age) inevitably overthinking everything and poorly hitting the ball.

All of the biblical one-anothers can feel like those golf instructions. It seems impossible to figure out which is the *most* important at any given moment. The Bible tells us to do *lots* of different things for one another, but how are we supposed to remember them all, let alone know which one to apply? This is why I've tried to summarize the one-anothers into the four simple memorable words that I introduced in chapter 2. Again, "gospel care is the God-exalting, grace-saturated art of loving another person, through patiently *knowing*, sacrificially *serving*, truthfully *speaking*, and consistently *applying the gospel* in order to help them become more like Jesus."

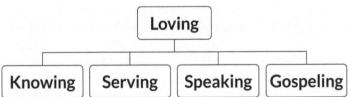

These are the four categories that we'll explore in the rest of this book. We're going to unpack each one of them, discuss a number of the one-anothers each word summarizes, and look at how we can apply them with those we are ministering to. But, as we do so, it's imperative for you to keep in mind just how easy it is to do a lot of things that *look* like gospel care, but aren't actually what God has called you to.

No Substitute

You see, in our sin-stained hearts there are numerous motivations other than love that can lead us to know others, serve others, speak to others, or even apply the gospel to others. You can ask questions, listen attentively, and truly get to know someone out of a self-serving desire to be "in the know." You can sacrifice your time or energy to serve someone because it makes you feel useful and important. You can speak truth into someone's struggle out of a sense of self-righteousness or self-congratulation that you know the "right" answer. You can quote a Bible verse to someone not necessarily because you *know* it's what is most needed, but because you'd feel guilty if you didn't say something "biblical," and you want to alleviate that guilt. You can even help apply the gospel to someone's heart out of a desire to *be* their savior, instead of pointing them *to* the Savior.

Back in 1 Corinthians 13, just before that famous description of love we looked at above, is Paul's equally famous assertion of the necessity of love. Again speaking of our relationships with one another in the body of Christ, he says,

> *If I speak in the tongues of men and of angels, but*
> *have not love, I am a noisy gong or a clanging cymbal.*
> *And if I have prophetic powers, and understand all*
> *mysteries and all knowledge, and if I have all faith,*
> *so as to remove mountains, but have not love, I am*
> *nothing. If I give away all I have, and if I deliver up my*
> *body to be burned, but have not love, I gain nothing.*
> *(1 Cor. 13:1–3)*

Love does not just benefit gospel care; it is absolutely necessary to it. The implications of what Paul says here are staggering. He is throwing into the trash all of our efforts to patiently listen to others, give money to others, or share Scripture with others that are devoid of authentic love. Now, of course he is not demanding that our hearts be perfectly pure (we will all continue to battle with the pull of self-love until the day we die). But he *is* clearly communicating the unequivocal expectation that our care and service for others must *always* contain authentic love for them.

Without love, it doesn't matter how sacrificial our service is or how theologically astute our words are. Without love, they are simply loud, annoying noises before the ears of the King. Without love, we are playing off-key and out of sync with the melody. Without love, we are ruining the song.

But *with* love, gospel care is a beautiful improvisational riff, blessing the recipient and glorifying the Creator. With love, we can step into the messes around us with confidence that God will use our imperfect efforts to bring about healing, repentance, freedom, and hope. With love, we have the one necessary qualification to engage in one another's messy lives and fulfill God's call to gospel care. And love, regardless of its many manifestations, *always* begins with listening.

ENDNOTES

1. Frederick M. Lehman, "The Love of God."
2. John Piper, *Desiring God*, 100.
3. Piper, *Desiring God*, 101.

CHAPTER 5

AN INTELLIGENT HEART

Knowing, Part 1

Jeff wouldn't stand out in a crowd. He's a short, mild-mannered, quiet, and respectful young man, and when we first met, he didn't seem all that different from any other visitor on a Sunday morning. After chatting on a couple of different occasions, Jeff and I decided to grab coffee during the week. So, on a typical Wednesday night, we met up at a local coffee shop.

We stood in line together, and after the coffee had been brewed and the milk had been steamed, I began looking for a table. After finding one I looked back to let Jeff know, but I could tell something wasn't quite right. His eyes were darting from side to side and his originally cheerful face had been overcome with nervousness. As soon as I got back to him, Jeff shyly asked if we could find somewhere more private. So we walked across the street to one of those strange urban parks that simply consist of art installations and benches, where we were sure we could be alone.

Our conversation was slow going. Jeff told me about the months he had spent showing up every Sunday and standing across the street from the movie theater where our church met, unable to get up the nerve to go in. He told me about some of his doubts and fears, and he described the anxiety he was feeling even as we talked. There were so many things I wanted to say to him, so many truths and passages that came to mind, but I could tell that I didn't have the whole story yet. Part of me wanted to start talking just to avoid the painfully slow pace of the conversation. But instead, I just kept asking questions and listening patiently.

Eventually Jeff quietly admitted, "I want to tell you something else, but I'm afraid to." I assured him of my care for him and then simply waited. It was at this point that Jeff began to unravel the incredibly messy story of the previous three years of his life. He had just recently been released from prison and was now trying to navigate a new life that involved a probation officer, court-mandated classes, employment as a felon, countless broken relationships, and the emotional impact of the previous few years. Jeff had become a Christian, but he barely knew what that meant in practice. It was all more than he knew how to handle. And the truth was, it was all more than I knew how to handle, too.

But the one thing I knew was that, to start with, Jeff needed someone who would listen to him. He needed someone who would take the time to understand his story. He didn't need someone who would offer him platitudes based on a partial understanding of his situation. He needed someone who would speak truth into the entirety of his messy and complex life. In other words, he needed what every person we minister to needs: he needed to be understood. It is this kind of understanding that lays the foundation for everything else we say and do in gospel care. That is why, in *every* relationship, before we speak or act, we first need to take time to truly know the person we're ministering to.

KNOWING IN LOVE

Whenever I first sit down with someone who is hurting or struggling, the same thought runs through my mind. It doesn't matter if it's someone I've just met or an old friend with a new struggle, the thought is always the same: "I have no idea what to say to you." This thought used to panic me. Here is a friend pouring out their heart, being vulnerable, and entrusting me with the details of their inner life, and I can't think of anything to say? What is wrong with me?

I've come to realize that not knowing what to say often isn't the flaw I was afraid it was. You see, when someone begins to open up about a deep struggle or a hurt, you *shouldn't* immediately know what to say. Too often we speak too quickly, without taking the time to fully understand the person we're talking to or the particular issue they're struggling with.

Proverbs warns about this exact thing:

> *If one gives an answer before he hears,*
> *it is his folly and shame.*
>
> *(Prov. 18:13)*

Speaking or acting before truly listening and understanding isn't an act of love—it's an act of folly. Love means listening to others carefully, seeking to understand them fully, until we *do* know what to say. Love listens patiently and prayerfully until it can confidently say, "I know exactly what to say to you." As the proverb continues:

> *An intelligent heart acquires knowledge,*
> *and the ear of the wise seeks knowledge.*
>
> *(Prov. 18:15)*

As we saw in the last chapter, gospel care is essentially a ministry of love. And love, if it truly seeks the best for the other person, is not applied arbitrarily but wisely and carefully. As David Powlison wrote, "Wise counseling [or any form of gospel care] is essentially a way of loving another person well. It is a way of speaking what is true and constructive into this person's life right now. Good [personal ministry] is essentially wise love in action."[1] I love that phrase "*wise love in action*." I'm not sure there's a more concise or accurate description of gospel care. And as we see from these proverbs, wise love is love that seeks and acquires knowledge. Wise love begins with knowing a person.

It must also be said that knowing a person is different from knowing *about* a person or *about* their problem. We're often content to learn some basic facts *about* a person or *about* their situation without taking the time to truly know the person as a unique, image-bearing individual. This is a clear indication that we're more captivated by the problem than we are by the person. And while that might be all right if you were the person's mechanic or physician, it falls far short of what you are called to as their friend. Love seeks to know the person.

We see this kind of knowledge-based love modeled repeatedly in the life of Jesus. While people came to him with all sorts of different attitudes, situations, and problems, he was never content to take them at face value. He was always after something deeper.

A Samaritan woman was seeking water when she met Jesus at a well, but he spoke to her out of a deep *knowledge* of her past and her greatest needs (John 4:1–26). A rich young man came to Jesus to justify himself in light of his seemingly godly life, but Jesus confronted him out of a *knowledge* of the deepest desires of his heart (Matt. 19:16–22). A paralytic was brought to Jesus in order that his most obvious problem might be addressed, but Jesus first forgave him out of a *knowledge* of his most fundamental problem (Matt. 9:1–7).

Now, even though Jesus possessed this deep knowledge more easily (and supernaturally) as one who was both fully God and fully man, we are still called to follow his example. For us, this deep personal knowledge is gained through *listening* patiently, *asking* good questions, *interpreting* what we're told in light of a biblical worldview, and then *considering* what the person needs most. These are the four components of knowing another person we're going to explore in the rest of this chapter and the next.

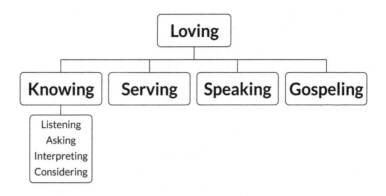

Listening, asking, interpreting, and considering are where we must begin in every loving relationship. The art of gospel care is built on the foundation of being intimately acquainted with God's Word *and* being intimately acquainted with the person we're ministering to. True love is wise and understanding love. And that kind of love begins with quiet listening.

LISTENING

The first service that one owes to others in the fellowship consists in listening to them. Just as love to God begins with listening to His Word, so the beginning of love for the brethren is learning to listen to them.[2]

When we love God, we want to listen to him in his Word. When we love others, we want to listen to them through their words. In his classic work on the basics of reading the Bible, Howard Hendricks summarizes the process of studying Scripture into three steps: observation, interpretation, and application.[3] And, as common sense would suggest, the order of these three steps is of critical importance. You can't apply Scripture correctly if you haven't interpreted it accurately. And, similarly, you can't interpret God's Word accurately if you haven't taken the time to observe it carefully. Just as knowing God through his Word begins with observing it carefully, so knowing another person begins with listening to them attentively.

Listening isn't easy. There are all sorts of dynamics that fight against good listening, both inside and outside of us. Self-focus is the most prominent internal enemy of listening. One of the main reasons we fail to listen well is because we're more focused on ourselves and how a person's story affects (or doesn't affect) us than we are on that person. Sometimes we end up tuning out because we no longer find what's being shared interesting. Other times we spend our mental energy figuring out how to respond instead of figuring out how to understand.

When we're distracted by trying to come up with a response, or simply waiting until we can unleash our scripted rebuttal, we cease to truly listen. This, again, is what makes discipleship such an improvisational art. We're meant to be fully present in the moment, listening intently, engaged with the other person, until we know the right notes to play.

But we're also fighting against external enemies of listening. Not only do our hearts make listening harder, but so does the fallen world we live in. We live in a world where some of the most popular forms of communication actually make us *worse* listeners. Just think about the number of words that pass through your mind on any given day: texts, social media posts, headlines, television, radio, podcasts, friends, coworkers, emails, books, articles, etc. We're consuming more information than ever before, but we're also cultivating the habit of hearing information and immediately forgetting it. While this may make us more efficient tweeters, it dulls our ability to truly listen.

LISTENING REQUIRES INTENTIONALITY

Genuine listening requires us to fight against this tide. We have to push back against the internal and external enemies of listening so that we can intentionally engage with people. We can't just assume that hearing someone's words means we're actually listening to them. Love requires more. In fact, listening is probably one of the hardest acts of love God calls us to. That is why listening requires intentionality. We're not going to listen well by accident. We need to make a concerted effort to listen well and to develop the character traits that strengthen our ability to listen.

What comes to mind when you think of good listening skills? I think of a list of practical tips I received in my Intro to Psych course in college. It included things like making eye contact, leaning forward, using verbal responses, and repeating what you've heard back to the person. Have you ever tried to apply tips like these? I have. I've sat with someone in a church office and looked into their eyes, leaned toward them with my elbows on my knees, made some well-timed "hmm"s and "uh-huh"s, and periodically responded with, "So it sounds like you're saying . . . " The only problem is, it didn't seem to make me any better of a listener. Instead of really listening, I was distracted by all the tips I was supposed to follow. And what's more, I probably looked like an intimidating, overly caffeinated counseling zealot as I stared this person down while they tried to open up and share.

This has led me to believe that good listening doesn't come as a result of following certain "tips" or even developing certain external skills. Good listening comes as the result of the character qualities that are the natural product of love— qualities like *intentionality* (as I just mentioned), *patience*, *compassion*, and *curiosity*.

LISTENING REQUIRES PATIENCE

When we genuinely love someone, we invest the time it takes to simply let them share, even when the sharing is inefficient, scattered, or confused. Now, I'm not saying that you should always let someone talk as much as they want to; there will inevitably be times when a person's talking is counterproductive. But in order to truly get to know someone, we must take the time to listen beyond an initial, basic sharing of facts. People aren't machines, and their minds don't work like a Google search. When someone is wrestling through hurts and struggles, we must create the space to let them mentally wander a bit so that we can truly get to know them *as a person*.

In addition, many issues, both in people's pasts and in their hearts, are more complex than can be explained or understood in one conversation. Getting to know people takes time. We can often be eager to offer a Bible verse and see people on their way instead of taking the time to really understand the multitude of factors that have contributed to their current situation.

It makes me think of a scene in Alan Paton's incredible work *Cry, the Beloved Country* shortly after two of the main characters, Kumalo and Msimangu, meet for the first time. Kumalo is from a small, far-off village. Msimangu lives in the big city, Johannesburg, where the scene takes place. They begin to talk about their unique experiences and the complex worlds in which they live, but then Msimangu stops the conversation short and simply says, "These things are too many to talk about now. They are things to talk over quietly and patiently."[4] This seems like a perfect sentiment for many of the messy moments when those we are ministering to are hurting and struggling. These "are things to talk over quietly and patiently."

LISTENING REQUIRES COMPASSION

But this kind of patience does not exist in a vacuum. Genuine patience always goes hand in hand with genuine concern and care. This is why listening also requires compassion. When we love someone, we will inevitably care enough about them to be both truly interested and emotionally moved. Since this was true of our Savior, it should be true of us as well. Jesus' compassion is unmistakable throughout the Gospels and is mentioned explicitly multiple times: "When [Jesus] saw the crowds, *he had compassion* for them, because they were harassed and helpless, like sheep without a shepherd" (Matt. 9:36); "And when the Lord saw her, he had compassion on her and said to her, 'Do not weep'" (Luke 7:13).

Jesus' love for those around him produced deep and emotionally engaged compassion. When we are emotionally engaged with those we're ministering to, we are present with them in a way that heightens our ability and desire to listen. On top of that, our listening makes us more insightful. Compassion gives us ears to hear the "question behind the question" or the "story behind the story." When we are both intellectually *and* emotionally engaged with someone, we gain a sensitivity that God uses to help us come to know them more fully. Not to mention the fact that genuine compassion produces an environment that encourages further sharing because people know that we really do care. "Put on then, as God's chosen ones, holy and beloved, compassionate hearts, kindness, humility, meekness, and patience . . . " (Col. 3:12).

LISTENING REQUIRES CURIOSITY

Lastly, if we are to truly help others understand themselves and their multifaceted trials (James 1:2) in the light of God's Word, listening requires curiosity. When we love someone intentionally, patiently, and compassionately, we are going to be interested enough to not only listen to what they share but to also wonder about the details they haven't yet shared. While pride assumes it knows a person before it has all the facts, humility recognizes there's always more to learn.

That leads us to the other side of the listening coin: asking good questions.

ASKING QUESTIONS

Have you ever met someone who is a really good question-asker? They tend to be the relationships that stand out to us. I had a good friend named Josh who was one of the best question-askers I'd ever met. He would ask the most insightful and thoughtful questions that would always draw people out. His conversations would inevitably veer from the mundane to the meaningful and they would allow him to build relationships like no one else I knew. So, I set out to try to become a good question-asker like Josh.

It may sound a little silly, but I began by studying Josh and his questions. I would try to categorize his questions or even memorize some of them. I even asked him about his questions, trying to figure out how he came up with them. And the more I dug, the more I realized that there really was a key difference between Josh and me.

The main difference between Josh's questions and mine was that Josh actually wanted to know the answers. It was his love-fueled curiosity that produced his Spirit-empowered creativity. He asked good questions because he truly desired to know more about the people he was talking with. I, on the other hand, wasn't primarily motivated by the answers I would hear. I just wanted to be a "good question-asker." I wanted that Christian badge to put on my vest. So I came to realize that the road to becoming a better question-asker wasn't paved with research. It was paved with repentance.

When we love those we're ministering to, it will produce in us a sanctified curiosity that longs to draw them out so that we might know them and understand their hearts better.

The purpose in a man's heart is like deep water,
but a man of understanding will draw it out.
(Prov. 20:5)

Our hearts are deep and complicated things. Think about how mysterious and unknown the depths of the ocean were when Solomon wrote that proverb. There were no submarines, no underwater cameras, no departments of oceanography. While Solomon owned a fleet of ships (1 Kings 9:26), very little was known about what actually took place in the deep ocean. Dolphins, whales, and other sea creatures would occasionally appear at the surface of the water, but what happened underneath was a mystery. The secrets of the deep waters of the ocean were completely unknown and undiscovered. *That* is how complicated and mysterious the purposes of our hearts are, Solomon says.

"But a man of understanding will draw it out." When we ask wise and loving questions with a desire to truly know one another, we can draw out the purposes and intentions of one another's hearts. We become like an early oceanographer exploring the ocean floor for the first time. While the early explorers of the depths of the ocean knew that different types of fish and sea plants existed, their explorations revealed species and subspecies that no one had ever seen before. In the same way, when we plumb the depths of someone's heart with wise and timely questions, we will discover forms of hurt, depression, fear, joy, beauty, and strength that are unique to that person. As we ask good questions, we get the privilege of knowing another person, uniquely created in the image of God, more and more.

So how do we become better question-askers? As I've said, I believe that good question-asking begins with a genuine desire to know the other person and a love-fueled curiosity that stokes our creativity. At the same time, some of us need practical guidance to help jumpstart that creativity, especially when we're out of practice. One of the ways people seek to get this kind of practical help is through lists of recommended questions. Maybe you'd like me to provide you with "The top fifty questions to ask in gospel care." But while lists like that can serve a purpose, I've never found them all that helpful in the real moments of life. Maybe it's because my memory isn't that great, or maybe it's my embarrassment at the idea of carrying a list of questions around in my pocket, but it just doesn't seem practical.

What I *have* found helpful, however, is thinking about questions in terms of broader categories. As we'll look at in depth in chapters 11 and 12, the Bible has a clear and simple (though not simplistic) explanation for what motivates everything we say, do, think, and feel. Put concisely, our *behavior, thoughts,* and *emotions* all stem from what the Bible calls our *hearts.* In addition, all of these behaviors, thoughts, and emotions inevitably take place in the context of our *circumstances.* To truly know a person, we need to be asking questions in all of these areas.

ASK CIRCUMSTANCE QUESTIONS: "WHAT HAPPENED?"

Circumstance questions are the questions we most commonly ask. We ask broad questions, like "How is work going?" and we ask specific questions, like "What did the doctor say?" But we shouldn't underestimate the importance of understanding the circumstances people are experiencing. Circumstances provide the broad and specific context for all of their behaviors, thoughts, and actions. In fact, we can't accurately understand a person's actions, or the motives behind those actions, without grasping the circumstances in which those actions took place.

Ask *Behavior* Questions: "What Did You Do?"

Behavior questions are the most obvious personal questions we can ask. They have clear answers. Actions either took place or they didn't. They're far more concrete than thoughts or emotions. This is where specificity is so important. When we get vague answers to discrete questions it provides the opportunity for more specific questions. Don't assume you know what a person means when they offer vague answers; make sure you know. If, for example, you ask someone how they are doing in the area of sexual purity, don't assume you know what the reply "Good!" means. To you, "good" might mean that they've stopped looking at porn. To them, however, it might mean that they are only looking at porn three times a week. There are countless different behavior questions that could be asked. Identify the ones that are the most important for knowing the person and their current struggle. Then take the time to make sure you fully understand the answers.

Ask *Thought* Questions: "What Were You Thinking?"

Now, of course, the tone of this question matters a lot. I don't mean to suggest that your response to others' actions should include screaming, "What were you thinking?"! What your response should include are questions that help you to understand their thought patterns. What we think about most reveals what our hearts are captivated by. When we spend our days repeatedly thinking about how much we hate our job, or about the house we wish we had, or about the ways that our spouse has disappointed us, it reveals something we're longing for; it points us back to the motivations of our hearts. Helping people to identify the patterns in their thought lives can help us to know them and understand their struggles in powerful ways.

ASK *EMOTION* QUESTIONS: "WHAT WERE YOU FEELING?"

Emotion questions aren't just for "emotional people." We're all emotional people, created in the image of a God who himself expresses emotions. Even the most logical and rational people I know can become quite frustrated when others aren't similarly rational or their logic breaks down. While the logic itself may be unemotional, the frustration is as emotional as it gets. Questions that help you to understand what others are feeling give you insight into both the circumstances they're experiencing and the heart motivations that produce their responses. When asking emotional questions, it's particularly helpful to ask about the past as well as the present. "Is this the first time you've ever felt that way?" "What has caused you to feel that way before?" "Do you feel that way often?" Asking about a person's past helps you to know and understand them even more fully, since who someone is today isn't just a set of facts but the result of a story.

ASK *HEART* QUESTIONS: "WHAT ARE YOU WORSHIPING?"

If we are to truly know one another and care for one another's souls, we can't stop short of asking the deepest questions: we have to ask heart questions. Heart questions are not only the hardest to ask, they can also be the hardest to think of. We're not going to get very far by simply asking someone, "What are you worshiping?" We'll probably get a blank stare and a confused, "I don't know" (just like when I ask my kids, "Why did you do that?"). We need insightful questions that help reveal a person's motives. We need questions that help us understand what people value and desire most and, *therefore*, what they worship. This is where an exception to my dislike of lists comes in. David Powlison was one of the most insightful observers of human beings I've come across, and he compiled a list of what he called "X-Ray Questions" that can help us develop creative and contextually appropriate heart questions.[5] Here is a sampling to give you an idea of what good heart questions might look like:

> *What do you seek, aim for, and pursue?*
> *What are your goals and expectations?*
> *What do you fear?*
> *What do you think you need?*
> *Where do you find refuge, safety, comfort, escape, pleasure, security?*

On whose shoulders does the well-being of your world rest?
Whom must you please?
What gives your life meaning?
What do you see as your rights?
Where do you find your identity?[6]

Hopefully you can see at this point that there are *lots* of questions to ask. Unfortunately, many of us get stuck in just one of these categories, so we end up asking only one type of question. Some of us tend to ask only circumstance questions, others only behavior questions, and others only emotion questions. But in order to truly know someone well we need to take the time to ask all these different kinds of questions.

Again, there's no script. There's no list of fifty questions to ask in every situation. But hopefully these categories will give you some guidance and help to expand the types of questions you tend to ask. If you're equipped with these categories and you have the love-fueled curiosity we talked about earlier, you'll be able to love others and get to know them in ways you never realized were possible. You'll hear the song like you've never heard it before. You'll be ready to play notes you never thought of playing before. You'll be engaging in the art of gospel care.

Still, listening and asking questions are just the first step. If we're truly going to help the person we're listening to, we also need to interpret what they are saying in light of a biblical worldview. How do all of the circumstances, behaviors, thoughts, emotions, and heart motivations fit together and relate to one another? How does Scripture describe what this person is experiencing? How does God teach us to conceptualize the hurt and the struggle we're hearing about? Where does this person need more of Scripture's light? Once we've listened, how do we lovingly respond?

ENDNOTES

1. David Powlison, *Speaking the Truth in Love*, 5–6.
2. Dietrich Bonhoeffer, *Life Together*, 97.
3. Howard Hendricks, *Living by the Book*.
4. Alan Paton, *Cry, the Beloved Country*, 56.
5. The full list of these questions has been published in at least two books (Paul David Tripp and Timothy S. Lane, *How People Change*; and David Powlison, *Seeing with New Eyes*), as well as in the *Journal of Biblical Counseling* 18, no. 1 (Fall 1999). It has also been widely reproduced on the Internet with permission.
6. Powlison, *Seeing with New Eyes*, 132–140.

CHAPTER 6

WHAT'S MOST NEEDED?

Knowing, Part 2

Jessica's anger was out of control. She had yelled at her entire community group (a group she helped lead) for a second week in a row and the pressure she was under had resulted in an obvious physical tic. Now one of her roommates had reached out asking for help.

Jessica was a high-performing college student and the only child of high-performing parents. She was a budding leader both in the church and in her on-campus ministry—her Christianity was yet another area she excelled in. While she could be intense at times, she generally engaged others with a great deal of compassion and wisdom. My wife, Lara, and I knew Jessica casually but hadn't spent much time with her. However, in light of everything that was happening, it was obvious that we should reach out.

After we had exchanged a few text messages, Jessica came over to our home late one night. Our kids had been successfully put to bed, so we all went out to the back patio and sat down to talk. Jessica explained what happened both in her community group and with her roommates, without sparing a detail. She then shared how she had recently been blowing up at her parents whenever she visited them, and how she could barely drive without wanting to swear at half the drivers on LA's insane freeways. It seemed obvious what needed to be said and what needed to be done.

Jessica needed the light of God's Word, so that's exactly what I provided—on full brightness! I shared about the seriousness of anger and how Jesus equated it with murder (Matt. 5:21–22). I talked about the danger of the tongue and how destructive our words can be (James 3:5-12). I talked about the importance of the sun not going down on our anger (Eph. 4:26). And I even spent some time exhorting her about the importance of honoring her parents (Ex. 20:12; Eph. 6:1-2). I knew Jessica understood the gospel and I knew that she had the Spirit of God dwelling in her, so I simply wanted to make sure she knew what God desired of her.

As I spoke, Jessica became more and more tense. She didn't look angry, but her tic got more frequent and severe. She would respond affirmatively when I asked if what I was saying made sense. But as we went on, her responses became increasingly short. Finally, she just burst into tears. She sobbed uncontrollably, and all she could say was that she didn't know why she was crying. She'd cry and then apologize and then cry some more. That's essentially how our time ended. By this time, it was after 11:00 p.m. and I didn't quite know what else to say. Lara graciously prayed for Jessica and then walked her out.

I made a lot of mistakes that night. I assumed I knew what Jessica needed before I ever really knew her or understood what was going on. I failed to take the time to understand all the factors that had contributed to her struggle. And instead of interpreting everything she was going through in light of Scripture, I looked for the first "scriptural" concept I could find and then ran with it. But the straw that broke the camel's back was my use of "honor," a concept with deep emotional ties that framed the cultural expectations she had inherited from her parents.

In addition, I did all of this without taking the time to build a genuine relationship with her and let her know that Lara and I truly did care for her. Our relationship wasn't strong enough to hold the weight I had loaded onto it. As a result, our relationship lasted one conversation; and just like that, it was over. Thankfully, the Lord had filled our church family with other women who knew Jessica and were more gentle, compassionate, and careful than I had been. Jessica had the chance to walk through her struggles with a couple of them, and she came to forgive me.

The scary part is that nothing I told Jessica that night was theologically inaccurate. It wasn't that I offered her the wrong truth; it was simply that I offered it at the wrong time and in the wrong way. As we will see, love speaks the right truth at appropriate times and in compassionate ways. This is why, before we open our mouths or jump into action, we need to take time to interpret what we've heard and consider what is most needed in each particular moment.

INTERPRETING IN LIGHT OF A BIBLICAL WORLDVIEW

As we listen and ask questions, we not only hear information and facts, we also hear interpretations. Everyone has a working theory for why they do what they do, why they think what they think, and why they feel what they feel. These theories are based on a mixture of anything from scientific studies to pop-psychology books; from psychological diagnoses to Facebook quizzes. They include things like birth order, personality type, unmet primal needs, and evolutionary drives. We love theories that attempt to explain why we do, think, and feel the way we do.

But as Christians, the question *we* must be asking as we seek to offer *gospel* care is, "What does *God* tell us is motivating what we do, think, and feel?" As I mentioned in the last chapter, Scripture teaches that "our behavior, thoughts, and emotions all stem from what the Bible calls our hearts. In addition, all of these behaviors, thoughts, and emotions inevitably take place in the context of our circumstances." Our circumstances provide the pressure that brings the realities of our hearts out into the open.

I've heard this explained with numerous different analogies, but my favorite is to think of the relationship between suffering (our fallen circumstances) and sin (our fallen hearts) as being like a water bottle.[1] If I were to take the top off a full water bottle and smash it between my hands, water would inevitably go spraying everywhere (see why I like this?). And if I were to ask you, "Why did water come spraying out of the bottle?," you would most likely answer, "Because you smashed the bottle." And in one sense you would be absolutely right. But that is not the only reason water came flying out of the bottle. The most fundamental reason is *because there was water in the bottle*. If the bottle had been full of air, no amount of smashing could have brought water out of the bottle.

In a similar way, suffering is the pressure that brings whatever is in our hearts out into the world through our behaviors, thoughts, and emotions. Suffering and sin both contribute in very real ways to the messes we find ourselves in. They contribute in different but interrelated ways to bring about what we do, think, and feel. We'll talk about the specifics of this in a few chapters. For now, it helps to simply see that Scripture provides us with categories to understand people's problems, hurts, and struggles.

As we listen carefully, the work of interpretation begins when we ask ourselves:

- In what way is this person suffering?
  ◊ From a fallen body?
  ◊ In a fallen environment?
  ◊ In a fallen culture?
  ◊ Among fallen friends/family?
- In what way is this person sinning?
  ◊ In self-focused behaviors?
  ◊ In self-focused thoughts?
  ◊ In self-focused emotions?
  ◊ In who or what he or she is ultimately worshiping?

This interpretation is an important first step in genuine gospel care. If we simply wanted to be a kind listening ear, accurately interpreting what we're hearing wouldn't be important. If we were called to nothing more than surface-level comfort, we wouldn't need to worry about this. But, as we've seen, God is calling us to something more. He's calling us to love others *in order to help them become more like Jesus*. And if we are going to do that, we can't just ask, "What is this person facing?" We also need to ask, "How does *God* view what this person is facing?"

Jesus the Interpreter

This kind of interpretation was a constant part of Jesus' ministry, as well as the ministries of the apostles. While examples of the interpretation itself cannot be explicitly found in Scripture (because interpretation happens internally), the tangible results of interpretation are obvious. One example can be found in Jesus' interaction with Mary and Martha.

> *Now as they went on their way, Jesus entered a village. And a woman named Martha welcomed him into her house. And she had a sister called Mary, who sat at the Lord's feet and listened to his teaching. But Martha was distracted with much serving. And she went up to him and said, "Lord, do you not care that my sister has left me to serve alone? Tell her then to help me." But the Lord answered her, "Martha, Martha, you are anxious and troubled about many things, but one thing is necessary. Mary has chosen the good portion, which will not be taken away from her."*
>
> *(Luke 10:38–42)*

Martha didn't tell Jesus she was anxious, and she didn't ask him for guidance about what she should be doing. All Martha did was complain about her sister. But Jesus was listening. Martha offered an interpretation to Jesus: "I'm doing the right thing and Mary is being lazy." But instead of uncritically accepting Martha's interpretation, Jesus stopped and (before he spoke) interpreted the information he had been given in light of a biblical worldview. As a result, he recognized that something very specific was needed, and it wasn't what Martha thought. What was most needed was for Martha to be corrected; to be invited to stop her busyness and enjoy his presence. But none of that would have come about without Jesus first listening and reinterpreting what Martha was saying. He listened to her and interpreted her situation because he loved her.

COMMON INTERPRETATION ERRORS

There are two ways to misinterpret that are particularly common among Christians. The first is when we simply adopt the world's interpretations. When we use secular labels and explanations to explain people's thoughts, behaviors, and emotions (like those described at the beginning of this section) all we will have to offer will be secular solutions. But when we interpret a person's circumstances and struggles in light of Scripture, we are preparing to offer that person the only true hope that exists in our world: the gospel. As Dietrich Bonhoeffer (whose father happened to be the head of psychiatry at the University of Berlin) put it:

> *The most experienced psychologist or observer of human nature knows infinitely less of the human heart than the simplest Christian who lives beneath the foot of the Cross of Jesus. The greatest psychological insight, ability, and experience cannot grasp this one thing: what sin is. . . . In the presence of a psychiatrist I can only be a sick man; in the presence of a Christian brother I can dare to be a sinner.*[2]

The second common error is even more insidious. Far too often, Christians use simplistic "biblicized" interpretations and pass them off as truth. These are interpretations that may have a grain of truth to them, and may even utilize Bible verses, but are applied carelessly and without wisdom. One of the most prevalent examples of this is when we assume that a problem someone is facing must simply be a result of their own sin. While our sin does have consequences, that does not mean that all the suffering we experience is a result of our own personal sin. This is the mistake that Job's friends made which left them immortalized as examples of "what not to do" in personal ministry. Most of the counsel that Job's friends offered could be summed up like this:

> *If iniquity is in your hand, put it far away,*
> *and let not injustice dwell in your tents.*
> *Surely then you will lift up your face without blemish;*
> *you will be secure and will not fear.*
>
> *(Job 11:14–15)*

Job's friends kept condemning him over and over, sharing half-truths (and sometimes even whole truths) about God that, while true in certain situations, simply didn't apply to Job. As a result, Job rebuked them multiple times with words that you and I should pray we never hear about our counsel:

> *As for you, you whitewash with lies;*
> *worthless physicians are you all.*
> *Oh that you would keep silent,*
> *and it would be your wisdom!*
>
> (*Job 13:4–5*)

The mistakes made by Job's friends ought to be a sobering cautionary tale (and required reading!) for every one of us as we engage in gospel care. Speaking the truth in love involves more than simply talking about God or quoting Bible verses. True love for others begins with saturating ourselves in the Word of God so that we might love him more, know him better, and understand ourselves more accurately. We need more than proof texts for our ministry to be truly biblical; we need a holistic understanding of suffering and sin and of God's faithful presence with us in the midst of it all.

CONSIDERING WHAT'S MOST NEEDED

Probably the most common question I get asked in phone calls, emails, classrooms, and all sorts of other contexts is something to the effect of, "What would you say to someone who . . . ?" People are always grappling with the complexity of the messiness around them and they're just looking for some guidance. They care about those in their lives who are struggling or hurting, and they simply want to know how to help. This section provides the answer to that question that I so often struggle to find the words to explain.

Since every person is different and every situation is unique, unfortunately there is no simple answer to the question "What would you say to someone who is struggling with PTSD and continues to have outbursts of anger?" or "What would you say to a person who is battling postpartum depression and is distraught over the loss of what she thought would be the happiest days of her life?" or "What would you say to someone who is addicted to porn and has tried everything to stop but nothing works?"

What I would say is that I would listen carefully and patiently to that person. I would ask the person questions and seek to learn as much about him or her as I could. I would strive to interpret what they told me in light of a biblical worldview. And, finally, I would consider what was most needed in each particular moment I spent with them. This consideration is the linchpin of loving gospel care. It is the layer of thought that connects what we've come to know with what we say and do. It doesn't require the most time or effort, but it is a vital part of ministering to others well.

THE BIBLICAL CALL TO CONSIDER

By "consider what's most needed" I mean that in every unique moment and opportunity we are called to not only identify what truth a person needs to hear, but also what specific truth that person needs to hear at that particular moment. At every point in time, we are called to not only identify what action could possibly bless a person, but, more specifically, what action would particularly bless that person right now. Instead of simply saying the first thing that comes into our minds or doing the first thing we feel the urge to do, love *considers* the situation, with all its messiness, and speaks or acts out of a conviction of what the person most needs at that particular moment.

The author of Hebrews shows us that it is this kind of consideration that is at the heart of our ministry of gospel care. We aren't simply to "stir one another up to love and good works" but to "*consider how* to stir one another up": "And let us *consider how* to stir up one another to love and good works, not neglecting to meet together, as is the habit of some, but encouraging one another, and all the more as you see the Day drawing near" (Heb. 10:24–25). "Let us consider" is the main verb of this sentence. The practical applications of "not neglecting to meet together" and "encouraging one another" are both the result of us considering how we can "stir one another up to love and good works," or, as I've been putting it, "help one another become more like Jesus."

When we don't take the time to consider what's most needed, our words and actions don't convey love, but disregard. As I mentioned before, love speaks the right truth and it speaks it at appropriate times and in compassionate ways. Proverbs provides an analogy that brings this point home:

Whoever blesses his neighbor with a loud voice,
    rising early in the morning,
    will be counted as cursing.

(Prov. 27:14)

Imagine someone standing outside your apartment at 3:00 a.m. yelling at the top of their lungs about what a great friend you are, how delicious your cooking is, and how great your new haircut is. Most of us would be annoyed to get a text to that effect at 3:00 a.m., let alone "a loud voice" (and we'd probably wonder about the sobriety of our friend). A public blessing loses its virtue when delivered at the wrong time. The content isn't the problem—the timing of the delivery is. The same can be true of our own words and actions. And they don't have to take place at 3:00 a.m. to be poorly timed.

But it's not just the timing of our gospel care that we need to take into consideration. Paul urges the Thessalonians to minister differently to different people depending on how they interpret each person's struggle: "And we urge you, brothers, admonish the idle, encourage the fainthearted, help the weak, be patient with them all" (1 Thess. 5:14). The Thessalonians' interpretation of whether a person was idle, fainthearted, or weak became the basis for considering whether that person should be admonished, encouraged, or helped. How they served and spoke to those in their spiritual family differed dramatically, depending on who they were ministering to.

If someone was idle, encouraging or even helping them would be unloving. They needed to be patiently exhorted to do for themselves the things that were their responsibility to do. Similarly, if someone was fainthearted, admonishment would simply crush them; but help wouldn't allow them to see that they had strength and ability of their own either. To love the fainthearted well required encouraging them. And while admonishing the weak would simply be cruel, encouraging them wouldn't be much better. The weak needed more than words; they needed help.

In the same way, we are called to consider what different people need most in each of the different moments we care for them. There are numerous different actions and words we can choose from (which we will explore in the coming chapters), but before we engage our hands or open our mouths we need to take the time to humbly and prayerfully consider both the individual and the context if we are going to truly demonstrate love.

How to Consider

So, what should we take into consideration? If considering what's most needed is the linchpin to our loving gospel care, how do we do it? While just taking the time to stop and prayerfully ask the question is more than half the battle, here are some ideas of the types of things you should consider as you prepare to sacrificially serve or graciously speak.

Consider Their Circumstances

Gospel care should always begin with a sense of triage. People aren't ever dealing with just one hurt or struggle but are simultaneously under a barrage that is inevitably impossible to completely untangle. What are the biggest issues this person is facing? How are those issues coloring everything else he or she is experiencing? When someone loses a child, the most loving thing to do may simply be to weep together (for a while). When someone is under the threat of an abusive spouse, your first action ought to be to provide physical safety. When someone is hounded by the physical pull of an addiction, detox will have to come before much of the needed heart work. Where each person is at in their journey and what else is going on around them should always determine the shape our love takes in any given moment. We need to make sure that we take a person's most prominent circumstances into consideration as we consider what's most needed.

Consider Their Capacity

There are several internal and external dynamics that determine a person's capacity. Ultimately, all of us are finite. We can't deal with all the issues we're facing at the same time. This is why, instead of trying to address everything we could possibly address in a person's life, we are called to consider what is *most* needed right now. For example, some people may be able to take their people-pleasing head-on. They may be ready to read books, complete practical assignments, memorize Scripture, and expose all the different ways their people-pleasing is shaping their lives. Others may not be ready (or have the time or energy) to take on such a large and intense project. Trying to get them to do so would simply push them away and leave them isolated and confused. Instead, they may simply be ready to explore why they are inordinately motivated by their boss's approval, and they may be willing to listen to a sermon on the subject and begin to read their Bible more consistently as they prepare to go to work. One size doesn't fit all, which is why we need to consider what's most needed.

CONSIDER THEIR COMMITMENT

If our goal in gospel care is to help others become more like Jesus, that means that they aren't completely like Jesus yet—and won't be this side of heaven. While we can't expect perfection out of those we minister to, it is fair to expect them to be committed to growing in Christlikeness. You can't help someone become more like Jesus who doesn't want to be. This is why Paul says that those who are idle need something drastically different than those who are weak.

Two different people may be in a similar situation, struggling with a similar sin or battling a similar doubt. But what determines the shape of our love for them isn't simply their situation, but their trajectory within that situation. Someone who is idle isn't committed to change, and therefore shouldn't be practically helped but admonished. On the other hand, someone who is weak yet similarly struggling should be offered help for the journey they've committed to travel. Again, how we respond is shaped by what we determine is most needed.

Does this all sound pretty overwhelming? Does it sound vague and subjective? As we've walked through this section, I can already hear you scrambling around looking for your script again. We're uncomfortable with the freedom of considering what's most needed. Instead, we want God to tell us clearly and unambiguously what to say and what to do. That's where the "What would you say to someone who . . . ?" question comes from. If God won't give us a straight answer, we try to find someone who will. But that is not the way God has designed his body to work.

Instead, he has called each of us to love one another *without* perfect knowledge and *without* complete understanding. What he has given to us instead is wisdom. Any robot can read a script, but God has given to us—those who have been created (and re-created) in his image—the gift of his wisdom to guide our lives and our ministry to one another. This is why we've found Proverbs so helpful throughout the last two chapters.

> *Blessed is the one who finds wisdom,*
> *and the one who gets understanding,*
> *for the gain from her is better than gain from silver*
> *and her profit better than gold.*
> *She is more precious than jewels,*
> *and nothing you desire can compare with her. . . .*
> *She is a tree of life to those who lay hold of her;*
> *those who hold her fast are called blessed.*
> *(Prov. 3:13–15, 18)*

As we minister to others, whatever the mess, our confidence doesn't come from knowing all the right answers or even knowing exactly what to say or do. As we seek to love others by faithfully getting to know them, and as we consider what they need most in any given situation, we can find our confidence in the faithful guidance provided by the wisdom of God. Remember the promise from James that I mentioned back in chapter 3: "If any of you lacks wisdom, let him ask God, who gives generously to all without reproach, and it will be given him" (James 1:5).

You are called to love by listening, asking questions, interpreting, and considering what's most needed. "Get it right" isn't on the list. Inevitably you will make mistakes, like I did with Jessica. But, thankfully, *you* are not the agent of sanctification in people's lives. That's the Holy Spirit's job. Yet, because of his overwhelming love for us, God has invited us to participate in the miraculous work of transformation he is doing in the lives of those around us. Our part is to be faithful listeners, question-askers, and interpreters who seek to love others from our limited and finite perspectives. And as we do so, we get a front-row seat to see him work miracles in people's lives.

But lovingly knowing the people we are ministering to is just the beginning. Genuine Christian love can't stay theoretical for long. It must be put into action.

ENDNOTES

1. I've heard this analogy numerous times verbally over the years. The origin of it is unknown to me.
2. Dietrich Bonhoeffer, *Life Together*, 118–119.

CHAPTER 7

MORE THAN A COUNSELOR

Serving, Part 1

We had just finished one of our Sunday evening classes and everyone filed out heading for home. Nelson uncharacteristically stayed behind. Once everyone had left, he spoke to me in a low voice. "Can we get together this week? Things are a little rough at home."

Later that week Nelson and I sat together at our church office. His explanation of what had happened was all over the place, but I was finally able to piece together the fact that he had visited some sort of sexting/flirting website, created an account, and indulged himself in the mess of online sexual gratification. This particular form of online indiscretion had taken place before, but this time was different. This time he got caught.

As you can imagine, things blew up at home. His wife, Rachel, was more hurt than she could have imagined. His unfaithfulness, dishonesty, and betrayal were unbearable to her, especially because of similar betrayals she had experienced in her past. He knew that she was particularly sensitive in this area of their life, but he did it anyway. She couldn't believe it.

A week later I sat down with Rachel and she was still fuming. She had decided to move out and had already signed the lease on an apartment. She couldn't stand to be in the same room as Nelson, let alone live with him or share a bed with him. I cautioned her against the implications of moving out, but stopped short of calling it sin. She agreed to meet together with me and Nelson weekly in order to process what had happened and attempt to take steps forward.

The road toward reconciliation was not a simple one. It was a complicated process that even left me, as their counselor, oscillating between incredibly encouraged one week and unclear how to proceed the next. Both of them experienced hurt, anger, frustration, sadness, and helplessness at times. Nelson's sin was significant, but it was really just the tip of the iceberg. There were numerous ways he had failed Rachel in his leadership of their family. Consequently, Rachel had become angry and bitter at Nelson, and catching him in *this* sin gave her all the justification she needed to rage against him and really make him pay.

However, God's grace in both Nelson and Rachel's lives proved to be greater than the magnitude of their sin against each other. Slowly but surely God began drawing them back toward one another. Gradually they began the process of reconciliation and were able to forgive one another as Christ had forgiven them. Rachel was able to forgive Nelson not only for his online infidelity, but also for his failure to lead his family toward Christ. Nelson was also able to forgive Rachel for her rage and begin to trust the grace she was extending to him.

But then came the issue of Rachel moving back in. She knew that she should move back into their house and there was a significant part of her that wanted to do so, but there was one last practical hurdle (at least according to Rachel). The house was a mess.

"I really don't want to be a princess," Rachel told me, "but the house is gross. I know I should move home, but it just makes me not want to be there even more." It was a fair point. Of course, a messy house is not a valid reason not to move home, but at this point I was simply trying to set them up to succeed, and a messy house was a legitimate hurdle. Nelson is not a dirty guy, but it was obvious that his idea of "sanitary" was a little different from Rachel's.

Nelson and Rachel both worked demanding full-time jobs, and their kids were in various different activities. Neither of them could figure out when they would be able to find time to go through and really clean the house in a way that would make it comfortable for Rachel. And moving back in just to clean up Nelson's mess was, understandably, a little too on the nose for Rachel. On top of all this, they were experiencing some real financial trouble because of the double rent they'd been paying for three months, so there was no way they could afford a housecleaner.

So I did the only thing that made any sense in this type of situation. I gave them $100 and told them to get a housecleaner in there that week. Of course, I could have offered to invite over someone from the church to clean the house for them, but I knew they weren't quite ready to accept that kind of intimate service. The money was, in that moment, what was most needed. In secular settings, money usually flows from the one being helped into the hands of the helper. But if gospel care is to reflect the servant-minister model of Christ, we should expect it to oftentimes flow the other way.

SERVING IN LOVE

Somehow, somewhere along the way, personal ministry became primarily a "talking" ministry. When we think about ministering to others, we usually picture two people sitting in an office or over coffee talking about life, issues, Scripture, God, and the gospel. And, while gospel care must involve listening and talking, it must also involve more. A quick survey of the one-anothers throughout the New Testament demonstrates that many of them aren't ministries of talking at all. Here's just a sampling of the exhortations to non-talking ministry:

○ Outdo one another in showing honor (Rom. 12:10).

○ Rejoice and weep with one another (Rom. 12:15).

○ Show physical affection for one another (Rom. 16:16).

○ Care for one another (1 Cor. 12:25).

○ Be kind to one another (Eph. 4:32).

○ Forgive one another (Eph. 4:32).

○ Submit to one another (Eph. 5:21).

○ Bear with one another (Col. 3:13).

○ Seek good for one another (1 Thess. 5:15).

○ Pray for one another (1 Tim. 2:1).

○ Be hospitable to one another (1 Peter 4:9).

In his first letter, Peter describes the ministries of service and of speaking as two sides of the same coin: "As each has received a gift, use it to serve one another, as good stewards of God's varied grace: whoever speaks, as one who speaks oracles of God; whoever serves, as one who serves by the strength that God supplies—in order that in everything God may be glorified through Jesus Christ" (1 Peter 4:10–11a). You may see this passage as saying that some people are called exclusively to "speaking" ministries while others are called exclusively to "service" ministries, but that can't be Peter's intent here. First of all, it would fly in the face of all the service-oriented one-anothers in the list above; and, second, it would fly in the face of the service-oriented one-another (show hospitality) applied to all Christians in the immediately previous verse (1 Peter 4:9).

When we don't prioritize serving one another in our gospel care, we subtly communicate that Christians shouldn't *need* help. They shouldn't *need* to be served. We communicate that all that is needed is information from the pages of Scripture and that we have better things to do with our time than watch someone's kids, help fix a leak, or give someone a ride. But as Dietrich Bonhoeffer wrote, "Nobody is too good for the meanest service. One who worries about the loss of time that such petty, outward acts of helpfulness entail is usually taking the importance of his own career too solemnly."[1]

Jesus himself set an example of the tangible, service-oriented ways we ought to love one another by humbly washing his disciples' feet. The time had come for him to demonstrate his power and Kingship through his death and resurrection, but instead of *talking* to his disciples about the importance of humility and tangible acts of service, Jesus *showed* them.

> *When he had washed their feet and put on his*
> *outer garments and resumed his place, he said to*
> *them, "Do you understand what I have done to*
> *you? You call me Teacher and Lord, and you are*
> *right, for so I am. If I then, your Lord and Teacher,*
> *have washed your feet, you also ought to wash one*
> *another's feet. For I have given you an example,*
> *that you also should do just as I have done to you.*
> *(John 13:12–15)*

Yet, even in light of such a powerful example, many of us have somehow gotten away from seeing acts of service as an integral part of personal ministry. We may have agendas, appointments, plans, resources, or curriculums, but they all tend to neglect the nonverbal parts of living life together. And we wonder why so many of our disciples know the right things to say but aren't actually living them out! Even if unintentionally, we've modeled for them a ministry (and a lifestyle) of nothing but words.

If we truly love those we are ministering to, we need to rectify this neglect. As we seek to love those we are ministering to through our actions as well as our words, that love will take many different forms. While space doesn't allow us to look at all of them here, I've chosen a sampling of action-oriented one-anothers that are particularly central to providing gospel care: *praying, pursuing, sharing, bearing,* and *forgiving.*

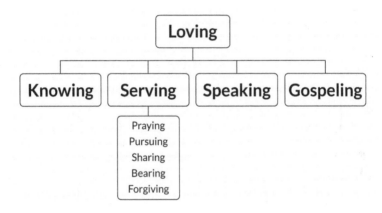

Each of these acts of service is just one aspect of gospel care. While the goal isn't to apply all of them continually (with the exception of prayer), each of them will probably be required at some point in most of our relationships. Each is a chord or note that may seem lifeless on its own, but becomes powerful when played at just the right moment with just the right strength in the context of the song of gospel care.

PRAYING

The greatest way we can serve others is to pray for them. It's so obvious that it probably goes without saying. But I'm afraid that too often that's exactly the problem. Not only does the reminder to pray often go unsaid, but the prayers themselves go unsaid as a result. And without prayer, we can't effectively love others the way God has called us to love them.

Devoid of prayer, gospel care can't be anything more than an external attempt at behavior manipulation. Additionally, gospel care without prayer cannot be considered "biblical," regardless of how many verses are quoted. To love the way Christ loved requires that we pray for one another.

When we serve others by praying for them, we acknowledge that it is not in our power to truly encourage, convict, or change them in any way (nor is it in *their* own power) apart from Christ. Through prayer, we appeal to the author and implementer of personal change, the Holy Spirit, acknowledging that all power for heart change comes as grace from him.

As I mentioned earlier, love begets service. And there is no action of service more loving than prayer. We see this fact demonstrated repeatedly in the life of the apostle Paul. A quick survey of his letters reveals how consistently he prayed for those he was ministering to.[2] D. A. Carson summarizes, "One of the remarkable characteristics of Paul's prayers is the large proportion of space devoted to praying for others."[3] Carson goes on to connect Paul's prayers with the heart of love that motivates this act of service: "If we learn to pray with Paul, we will learn to pray for others. We will see it is part of our job to approach God with thanksgiving for others and with intercessions for others. In short, our praying will be shaped by our profound desire to seek what is best for the people of God."[4]

In order to love others well, we must be in the habit of praying for them sincerely and consistently. Are you in the habit of regularly seeking what is best for the people in your life? Or do other motives subtly slip in and water down your prayers or supplant them altogether? Over the years I have found a few simple questions helpful in evaluating my own prayer life, particularly as it applies to my intercession for others:

1. What am I regularly praying for when I pray for others?
    ◊ Circumstances?
    ◊ Emotions?
    ◊ Behaviors?

◊ Thoughts?

◊ Heart-Motives/Desires?

2. What keeps me from praying for others?

3. What am I relying on to bring about transformation in those God has called me to minister to?

◊ My words spoken *to* the person?

◊ My words spoken to God *about* the person?

We are all tempted—more often than we'd care to admit—to believe that prayer isn't completely necessary. Many of us have seen God use our words or actions to bring about change in someone's life apart from our prayers. And instead of marveling at God's grace, we end up quietly impressed by our own abilities. This subtle pride usually lasts until we get into a situation where we feel in over our heads, and then we turn back to God for the extra bit of power we feel we need.

The problem is, God isn't some expert in the sky who steps in when we have reached the end of our abilities. He is the source of our abilities. We can't do anything on our own; we are completely dependent upon him. Whenever we begin to forget this fact, our prayer for others fades along with it.

> *W*hen there is little awareness of real need there is little real prayer. Some circumstances drive us to our knees. But there are periods when life seems quite manageable. Although Jesus said, "Apart from me you can do nothing" (John 15:5), this truth hits home more forcefully at some times than at others. In pride and self-sufficiency we may live for days as though prayer were needed only when something comes along that's too big for us to handle on our own. Until we see the danger and foolishness of this attitude, God's expectation for us to pray may seem irrelevant.[5]

When we see the foolishness of our self-sufficiency, a passion for prayer is the natural response. This is why Paul's letters are so saturated with prayer. It's not because he was so disciplined or because he felt guilty about needing to pray more. Paul's ministry was steeped in prayer because of his constant awareness that, while apart from Christ he could do nothing (John 15:5), through Christ he could do everything (Phil. 4:13).

Jesus taught his disciples to pray for his kingdom to come and for his will to be done on earth as it is in heaven (Matt. 6:10). There is simply no way to love someone better than to pray that God's kingdom would be made manifest more and more in their heart. If you don't know where to start, you could begin by echoing one of Paul's prayers:

> *I bow my knees before the Father . . . that*
> *according to the riches of his glory he may grant*
> *you to be strengthened with power . . . so that*
> *Christ may dwell in your hearts through faith—*
> *that you . . . may have strength to comprehend*
> *with all the saints what is the breadth and length*
> *and height and depth, and to know the love of*
> *Christ that surpasses knowledge, that you may be*
> *filled with all the fullness of God.*
>
> *(Eph. 3:14–19)*

Just as God's will is being perfectly carried out in heaven, we have the opportunity to contribute to his will being increasingly carried out here on earth. And the primary means of that contribution is not in what we say to those we're ministering to, but in what we say to God on their behalf. To love others well, we *must* pray for them.

Pursuing

A second way in which we are called to serve others is by pursuing them. My first formal ministry role in a church was when I was hired as a college ministry intern. I was given $500 a month, and I couldn't believe how lucky I was that someone was actually *paying* me to do ministry.

On my first day on the job I was handed a list of guys who were in the college ministry, and this became my "discipleship assignment." I was to contact them, get together with them, and begin life-on-life discipleship with each one of them. So that's just what I did. But I quickly realized that in order to keep up these relationships, I had to keep regularly reaching out to each one of these guys. It was much less common that they would call or reach out to me.

During this initial season in ministry, I remember looking forward to the day when I would be a "real pastor" because then people would call *me*, and I wouldn't have to spend part of a day each week following up with people that I hadn't heard from. Well, I've been a bona fide "real pastor" for a decade and a half now, and I still spend time every week following up with people who have gone silent.

While I do get a lot more calls and emails now than when I was an intern, when it comes to the people God has called me to minister to, I have found that loving, patient pursuit is an integral part of my gospel care of others. People reach out to you for all sorts of different reasons, but when those you are called to love go silent, it's oftentimes the moment they need your help the most.

Love is not passive. Love doesn't wait to be called or asked. Love is proactive and intentional. Love is demonstrated by knowing someone well enough to not need step-by-step instructions. Jesus demonstrated this kind of pursuit throughout his earthly ministry. While he did answer questions and respond to requests, by and large his mode of ministry was proactive. The Twelve became disciples not because they asked Jesus if he would mentor them, but because Jesus told them, "Follow me."

Whether it was Zacchaeus, Peter, the Samaritan woman at the well, or Levi the tax collector, Jesus pursued a relationship with many of the people he ministered to. Each of those relationships was unique, but they had one core dynamic in common: pursuit. Jesus initiated each relationship, and those that continued were maintained by his intentional, consistent investment. In light of this example, when Jesus left the Eleven with the parting instruction to "go therefore and make disciples," they must have understood discipleship as a proactive pursuit.

Similarly, we must see gospel care as an intentional, proactive call as well. Loving someone well will always involve pursuing them, especially when they are struggling or hurting. Personal ministry does not end when someone stops calling or stops showing up to regular meetings. In fact, this is oftentimes the moment when the most consequential kind of personal ministry begins.

Pursuit can take many different forms. Often it involves simply sending an email or a text. At times it may involve dropping by someone's home or place of work (when appropriate). It may even be accompanied by some other act of service like providing a ride or dropping off groceries. But inevitably, pursuing others will involve you stepping out of your comfort zone and stepping into the world of the other person simply so that you may have the opportunity to love them.

When evaluating the specific ways God has called me to pursue others, I have found it incredibly helpful to first ask the "who?" question. Who, specifically, should I be pursuing? This seems like an obvious and potentially unnecessary question, but the clarity it can bring is vital to obeying God's call to gospel care.

On the one hand, if you try to write down the names of those you are called to pursue and can't come up with a single name, you're probably not being faithful to God's call to love and minister to others. However, since you're reading this book, that's probably not your issue. The more common problem is that many of us think we are supposed to be pursuing far more people than we have the capacity to minister to. When we're asked the "who?" question, deep down inside we sometimes assume that the answer is "Everyone!" But when you spend a season in life answering this question with "Everyone!," you will inevitably spend the following season in life answering it with "No one!" You will end up burnt out. This kind of radical pendulum swing is not what God has called us to. We are finite beings called to sacrificial, yet finite, ministry.

Stop for a second and write down some actual names. Who has God called you to pursue? Don't try to do this in your head. You need to actually write down the names so you can see them all on the same piece of paper. Don't worry . . . I'll wait.

How long is your list? Five people? Ten people? Twenty people? Thirty people? Let's go back to the example of Jesus for a second. Jesus had all day, every day, available to minister to others. He didn't have a day job, a wife, or kids. While he taught and healed thousands, when it came to ongoing personal ministry, he dedicated himself to "discipling" only twelve. And of those twelve, he engaged even more specifically and deeply with only three.

If the God of the universe became a man and limited himself to that kind of direct, limited impact, why are we surprised when we exhaust ourselves trying to minister deeply to more people than he ever did? This isn't an issue of boundaries, strategies to avoid burnout, or even self-care. It's simply an issue of perspective. You and I are finite. God has not called us to minister to everyone all the time. *He* is infinite. *He* is inexhaustible. We are not. We are simply called to steward the limited time, energy, and resources God has given us for the good of those around us.

SHARING

Sharing our time and possessions with those we are ministering to is a third way in which we are called to lovingly serve them. This has been a hallmark of the church from the beginning. We see this displayed, famously, in the first days of the church as recorded in Acts 2. People were so transformed by the good news of Jesus that it changed everything about their lives:

> *And they devoted themselves to the apostles'*
> *teaching and the fellowship, to the breaking of*
> *bread and the prayers. And awe came upon every*
> *soul, and many wonders and signs were being done*
> *through the apostles. And all who believed were*
> *together and had all things in common. And they*
> *were selling their possessions and belongings and*
> *distributing the proceeds to all, as any had need.*
> *(Acts 2:42–45)*

Unfortunately, this description of life in the early church is more often used as an indictment of other Christians than as an encouragement to deeper community. I have heard countless Christians lament the fact that their experience of church hasn't looked like Acts 2. They find all sorts of reasons for this failure, but it always seems to be someone else's fault. Maybe you feel that way. But what if you and I stopped lamenting the failure of the church to perfectly mimic what God did in Jerusalem in those early days, and instead focused on exemplifying the model of our early church ancestors?

Generosity is one of the simple, practical ways we can seek to follow the example of the early believers in Acts. Acts 2:45 tells us that the early Christians weren't generous because they were duty bound, or in order to assuage a feeling of guilt for having been blessed with possessions. They were simply so transformed by the love and generosity of God that they wanted to love and be generous to others. As a result, all that God had given them was available for others as the opportunity or need arose. Paul encouraged similar generosity when he addressed "the rich" (read: you and me) in his letter to Timothy: "As for the rich in this present age, charge them . . . to do good, to be rich in good works, to be generous and ready to share, thus storing up treasure for themselves as a good foundation for the future, so that they may take hold of that which is truly life" (1 Tim. 6:17–19).

I love that phrase "generous and ready to share." It helps us see that our sharing and sacrifice aren't meant to exist in a vacuum (sharing for the sake of sharing), but instead are to take the shape of eager generosity; being "ready to share." It's as though our possessions are an arrow and we are to live with them constantly drawn in our bow, ready to deliver what we have to others as the need arises.

This is why "sharing" is another essential way in which we are called to serve those we minister to. If we are daily living our lives with a readiness to share, it is only natural that we will share with those we are ministering to.

Of course, what we share will inevitably be tied to what God has given us. Some of us will share our possessions because God has entrusted us with space or resources. Some of us will share our money because God has entrusted us with more than we require. Some of us will share our energy because we have been entrusted with certain abilities. But all of us can share our time since we have each been given the same twenty-four hours in a day to steward for the glory of God and the good of others.

Over the years, I have seen this take many different forms. Sharing may look like buying a meal, lending a car, watching some kids, forgiving a debt, or inviting someone to live with you for a time. It may take a few minutes or it may last a few years. But this is what gospel care entails. As we consider what is most needed in any given moment, the answer will often include the sacrificial sharing of what God has given to us.

This doesn't mean that we should give carelessly or without wisdom. Appropriate limits should be set, as many brothers and sisters may, in their sin, take advantage of this kind of generosity, as Paul warned (2 Thess. 3:6–12). However, limits should be determined using wisdom on a case-by-case basis.

This ought to lead us back to the importance of first "knowing" those we're ministering to. We cannot share wisely and lovingly if we haven't first taken the time to know a person and understand their circumstances. There is a big difference between the giving-in-knowledge that takes place in a committed ongoing relationship and the giving-in-ignorance that takes place when handing a $5 bill to the guy on the freeway off-ramp. One is discipleship, the other is (possibly) enabling. Yet, somehow, we are more likely to provide a meal for the man on the street than we are for the woman in the counseling room. The divorce of sacrificial sharing from gospel care simply doesn't make any sense. It may reflect a therapeutic model of personal ministry, but it has no resemblance to biblical love.

In his first letter, the apostle John tied the definition of love specifically to sacrificial generosity. Selflessness defined Christ's love for us, and it should define our love for one another:

> By this we know love, that he laid down his life
> for us, and we ought to lay down our lives for
> the brothers. But if anyone has the world's goods
> and sees his brother in need, yet closes his heart
> against him, how does God's love abide in him?
> Little children, let us not love in word or talk but
> in deed and in truth.
>
> (1 John 3:16–18)

To have what a person needs and *not* provide it is not just unloving, it's unbiblical. In all our relationships, we are called to reflect the sacrificial love of Christ not only in our words but in our actions as well. It may be something as simple as giving $100 for a housecleaner, or it may be something as complicated as adoption into your earthly family. Gospel care is not a safe or comfortable endeavor. Love may cost you. It most assuredly cost Jesus.

Brothers and sisters, you are *more* than mentors. You are *more* than disciplers. You are *more* than counselors. You are loving friends and representatives of Christ. You are the bearers of Christ's love in a lost and hurting world. You are spiritual family. Let us not love in word or talk but in deed and in truth.

ENDNOTES

1. Dietrich Bonhoeffer, *Life Together*, 99.
2. Rom. 1:9–10; 1 Cor. 1:4; Eph. 1:16–17; Phil. 1:3–4; Col. 1:9.
3. D. A. Carson, *A Call to Spiritual Reformation*, 66.
4. Carson, *A Call to Spiritual Reformation*, 75.
5. Don Whitney, *Spiritual Disciplines*, 70.

CHAPTER 8

WHEN THE *Mess* SPILLS ON YOU

Serving, Part 2

It was New Year's Day. I was relaxing at my house with football on the TV, spending some low-key time with our kids and beginning to take down all the Christmas decorations. It had been an intense year in a number of different ways, and while I'm not that into New Year's resolutions, the day felt new and fresh and exciting as we looked forward to the year ahead.

Rachel had moved back into her house about a month before, just in time for the holidays, and she and Nelson seemed to be doing better. Things weren't perfect but they were in a much better place than they had been. They'd spent a nice Christmas together as a family and they seemed to be settling into a new kind of normal. Which is why I was so surprised when my phone rang that afternoon and it was Nelson calling.

I picked up the phone and walked out of the house. He might have been calling simply to say, "Happy New Year!" but I doubted it. Nelson's voice was low but matter-of-fact. "I blew it last night. I was up late for the New Year, I'd probably had more beers than I should, and I went out on the back patio, opened up my computer, and started looking at porn." He explained how Rachel had caught him again, how ugly it had gotten, and how distraught he'd been all day.

He told me that he'd spent the morning going on a long walk and that, as he reflected, he had come to realize that he really did have a problem. But it wasn't just that he had a porn problem (although that was part of it), he had a drinking problem as well. He seemed to be mastered by both of them and, throughout his entire struggle with porn, they were undeniably related. He hadn't been completely honest about the seriousness of his struggle, even with himself. In fact, he hadn't been completely honest about a number of things.

There was a part of me that was happy for Nelson's new insight and confession. There was a part of me that was heartbroken for Rachel and having to endure this again after moving back in. But most of me was simply frustrated and discouraged. Not only had my beautiful, refreshing day off with my family been plunged into messiness because of Nelson's decisions the night before, but I had asked Nelson repeatedly and specifically about his drinking in the past. On multiple occasions I had broached the subject and tried to get more information, but he had always minimized it and never let me know of the full extent.

On top of all this, we had also sat in my office just before Rachel was to move back into their house, and I had looked Nelson in the eye and asked him explicitly, "Is there any other porn use that has taken place over the past few months while we've been meeting?" I told him firmly and clearly, "Now is the time to come clean. It will only get harder from here on. There can't be *anything* that Rachel has to find out about that she doesn't know now." We were striving to rebuild trust in their relationship, and he had been given one last chance to lay everything on the table. He told me that I knew *everything*.

Now, in addition to the drinking revelation, Nelson was on the other end of the line telling me that he hadn't told us the whole truth about his engagement with porn either. I listened dumbfounded as he told me that he had actually indulged in porn three or four times during the months we had been meeting but never said anything about it. I was coming to realize that Nelson had looked me square in the face and lied to me when he told me that I knew everything. Not only was Nelson's trust with Rachel broken, his trust with me was broken, too.

Nelson's sin was first and foremost against God. But he had also sinned against his wife and his kids. And now, simply because I had stepped into their lives to try to help, he had sinned against me. What a mess. But, as I mentioned in chapter 1, this shouldn't be all that surprising. Every person we minister to is messy. And it only makes sense that inevitably that mess is going to spill on us, too.

BEARING

Sometimes the mess of those we're ministering to takes the form of outright sin. People sin against us, like Nelson sinned against me, and God calls us to forgive. We'll look at this call to forgive in the next section. But sometimes the mess doesn't come in the form of sin. Instead, it shows up in the form of the quirks and weaknesses that every person on earth possesses. Maybe the person you're ministering to has never developed time management skills, so they always seem to show up late. Maybe the person has an overly sensitive conscience that affects when or where you can meet. Maybe they have different political views than you do. Or maybe the person just chews with their mouth open. In situations like these, forgiveness isn't the answer. Instead, God calls us to bear with them:

> *I therefore, a prisoner for the Lord, urge you*
> *to walk in a manner worthy of the calling to*
> *which you have been called, with all humility*
> *and gentleness, with patience, bearing with one*
> *another in love, eager to maintain the unity of the*
> *Spirit in the bond of peace.*
>
> *(Eph. 4:1–3)*

In this turning point in the book of Ephesians, Paul explains that our calling, as those redeemed by Christ, is to live humbly, gently, and patiently with one another. And one of the key trademarks of our patience toward one another will be our consistent willingness to "bear with one another in love." As one commentator puts it, "The Christian life is a life of putting up with other people, and this tolerance finds its ability and motivation in love."[1]

When we genuinely love another person, it will manifest itself in our readiness to tolerate annoyances and overlook irritations. This is what it means to "bear with one another." In a fallen world filled with messy and fallen people, we will inevitably find something annoying or irritating in every relationship. Of course, some relationships will prove to be more aggravating than others—but there is no limit to the patience we're called to have. As John Calvin affirmed, "Where love is strong and prevalent, we shall perform many acts of mutual forbearance."[2]

But annoyances aren't the only thing we're called to bear with. While the gospel produces spiritual strength and freedom from the shackles of guilt and shame, many of the people we minister to may have not yet developed that strength or freedom. Their consciences will be overly sensitive and their hearts will often be overwhelmed with guilt. As a result, we should be prepared to bear with weakness and sensitivity in every gospel care relationship. When we minister to those with more sensitive consciences or more fragile faith, we're called to look beyond our own consciences and desires. We are called to consider them, love them, and bear with their sensitivity.

> We who are strong have an obligation to bear
> with the failings of the weak, and not to please
> ourselves. Let each of us please his neighbor for
> his good, to build him up. For Christ did not please
> himself, but as it is written, "The reproaches of
> those who reproached you fell on me."
> (Rom. 15:1-3)

As we seek to embody the love of Christ toward those we are ministering to, patient "bearing with" is fundamental. Christ has been infinitely more patient with you than you will ever be asked to be with anyone else. He has borne with your forgetfulness, your distractedness, and your finiteness. He has borne with you through the busyness of school, the confusion of hormone changes, and every one of your unhelpful habits. And so, if we are to love others the way that he has loved us, we need to bear with them, too.

If someone feels strongly about a strict keeping of the Sabbath or giving up a certain luxury for Lent, we ought to facilitate our relationship in ways that make those things possible. While many American Christians may not experience tensions over what they eat, they may very well experience them over what they drink. Our enjoyment of alcohol is a keen example of an area we ought to take into consideration as we bear with those who are weaker or tend to have more sensitive consciences. As Paul wrote leading up to the passage I quoted above,

*Therefore let us not pass judgment on one
another any longer, but rather decide never to
put a stumbling block or hindrance in the way
of a brother. I know and am persuaded in the
Lord Jesus that nothing is unclean in itself, but
it is unclean for anyone who thinks it unclean.
For if your brother is grieved by what you eat,
you are no longer walking in love. . . . So then let
us pursue what makes for peace and for mutual
upbuilding.*

(Rom. 14:13–15, 19)

Before we move on, let's make this practical. What are some of the things you have a hard time bearing with? We all have them. Maybe they're weaknesses or sensitivities that friends of yours have that you would rather not have to take into consideration. Maybe they're the social quirks that you have a hard time overlooking. Maybe they're just your pet peeves. How might genuine, Christ-shaped love lead you to bear with others when those you're called to love are a source of irritation?

Or to get even more specific, who are the other Christians in your life you have a hard time bearing with? Picture them in your head. Don't worry, I won't tell them. What does love toward that person look like? How might your unwillingness to bear with them be limiting your opportunities to love them? What opportunities might open up if you chose to bear with them in love?

And maybe for a helpful perspective, what are some of the ways in which your friends and family have to bear with you? After all, you've got plenty of issues yourself. Every one of us is a mess. And while we are called to bear with the annoyances and weaknesses of others, they will inevitably have to bear with our annoyances and weaknesses as well. Bearing isn't a one-way street; Paul's call is for us to "bear with *one another* in love." But if we are to genuinely and practically love those God has called us to minister to, this kind of patient forbearing must begin with us.

FORGIVING

As we've seen, genuine love bears with the annoyances and weaknesses of those we're discipling or caring for. But when they sin against us, something more is required. The pain and relational damage caused by sin requires something greater. For that, forgiveness is needed. This is why, in a passage we've looked at previously, Paul stresses the importance of forgiveness *in addition to* bearing with one another: "Put on then, as God's chosen ones, holy and beloved, compassionate hearts, kindness, humility, meekness, and patience, bearing with one another and, if one has a complaint against another, forgiving each other; as the Lord has forgiven you, so you also must forgive" (Col. 3:12–13).

Bearing with one another is the way God calls us to deal with annoyances and weaknesses. Forgiveness is how God calls us to deal with sin. When the person you are ministering to lies to you, like Nelson did to me, forgiveness is what's needed. When they take advantage of your kindness or manipulate you, forgiveness is what's needed. When they gossip about you, or complain about you behind your back, or treat you like an enemy when you've tried so hard to love them, forgiveness is what's needed.

Sin is a big deal. It can't simply be overlooked or denied. When someone sins against us, the relationship is broken and requires reconciliation. This is why it hurts so much to be sinned against. While some of us like to act tough and pretend that we're not bothered by sins committed against us, our deep and brooding emotions inevitably betray the reality of our hearts. Whether we respond in instant, explosive anger or silent, simmering bitterness, the emotional effects of being sinned against are always present. And so are the relational effects. Somehow we can't just "get over it." We can't just "go on like normal." Something more is needed. Which is why God calls us to grant forgiveness.

DEFINING FORGIVENESS

But what is forgiveness? If you were to try to write down a definition of what you mean when you tell someone "I forgive you," what would it include? Over the years, I've found that most

Christians have a really hard time with that question. Some don't really know how to put it into words. Most simply end up repeating the definition provided by the self-help obsessed world we all live in.

The world around us defines forgiveness as something that you need to do for yourself. It's an internal, feelings-based reality that is to be pursued for the sake of personal inner health. We forgive because it's good for us. Forgiveness, then, is about avoiding bitterness, healing emotionally, and pursuing inner wellness. While I'd be the first person to desire your emotional health, inner wellness, and avoidance of bitterness, there are several problems with defining forgiveness this way.

First, when forgiveness is all about my own good, it is no longer an act of love. When forgiveness is defined therapeutically it becomes an act of self-love and ceases to be a part of God's call to genuinely and sacrificially love one another. This definition of forgiveness is completely out of sync with Paul's list of instructions in Colossians 3:12–13, all of which are others-focused.

What's more, this therapeutic definition of forgiveness doesn't line up with the way God forgives us. When God says that through faith in Christ we are completely forgiven, he is not saying, "You know, I've thought about it, and I don't want to hold on to this negative emotion any longer, so I'm going to let it go." He's not saying, "This bitterness is eating me up inside so I really just need to move on and forgive you." He's not saying, "I used to be angry but I've cooled down now, and so I'm ready to forgive you." If we're going to correctly understand how God calls us to forgive one another, we need to remember what it means that he has forgiven us.

Chris Brauns provides helpful definitions of both God's forgiveness of us and our forgiveness of one another in his excellent resource *Unpacking Forgiveness*. He defines God's forgiveness of us this way:

God's Forgiveness: A commitment by the one true God to pardon graciously those who repent and believe so that they are reconciled to him, although this commitment does not eliminate all consequences.[3]

Upon the foundation of the sacrificial work of Christ on the cross, God offers us the opportunity to be completely reconciled to him through the gracious pardoning of our sin (having the slate wiped completely clean) through repentance and faith. Our reconciliation to God doesn't necessarily do away with all of the consequences of our sin. Christ still had to pay the price and the penalty for it, and there may still be residual effects in this world. But our relational reconciliation can be complete because he has committed to not hold our sin against us any longer.

Now, if that is what God means when he says, "I forgive you," and we are called to forgive one another "as the Lord has forgiven [us]," then our definition of forgiveness should, obviously, echo his. In an attempt to draw this parallel, Brauns defines the forgiveness we are called to grant one another this way:

> [*Our*] *Forgiveness: A commitment by the offended to pardon graciously the repentant from moral liability and to be reconciled to that person, although not all consequences are necessarily eliminated.*[4]

This is what God means when he instructs us to forgive. *This* is how we can be genuinely reconciled to those who sin against us. *This* is how God calls us to deal with the mess of sin. So let's take this definition one piece at a time.

Forgiveness Is a Commitment

As Ken Sande writes in *The Peacemaker*, "Forgiveness is not a feeling. It is an act of the will."[5] Forgiveness is a choice we make, sometimes even in spite of our emotions. While our emotions are inevitably a part of the process, our willingness to make the choice to forgive often lays the groundwork for our emotions to come along over time. Being sinned against can be incredibly painful, but there is no hope of truly healing from that pain without committing to no longer hold that sin any longer against the one who committed it. This begins internally, as we choose to let go of the bitterness caused by dwelling on the sin, and then becomes external, as it shapes how we treat the person and talk about them with others. Sande summarizes the commitment of forgiveness in these four promises:

○ I will not dwell on this incident.

○ I will not bring up this incident again and use it against you.

○ I will not talk to others about this incident.

○ I will not let this incident stand between us or hinder our personal relationship.[6]

FORGIVENESS IS FOR THE REPENTANT

While God offers his forgiveness to everyone, he actually forgives only those who genuinely ask for it. Asking God for forgiveness requires us to confess our sin and express our intention to turn away from it. It's only through this genuine repentance that we can be reconciled to God. And it's only through genuine repentance that we can be reconciled to one another. Jesus makes this quite clear when he instructs his disciples: "Pay attention to yourselves! If your brother sins, rebuke him, and *if he repents*, forgive him, and if he sins against you seven times in the day, and turns to you seven times, saying, 'I repent,' you must forgive him" (Luke 17:3–4).

The reason repentance is required for forgiveness to be granted is because forgiveness is not internal but relational in nature. Forgiveness has a larger purpose than assuaging guilt— which leads to the next part of the definition.

FORGIVENESS IS FOR RECONCILIATION

The ultimate purpose of God sending his Son to die in our place was not just so that we can be pardoned from our sin. God is not a conflicted judge who wants to find a way to set his favorite defendants free. God is a loving Father whose relationship with his children has been broken by their sin. He sent his Son so that he could be reconciled to his children. Reconciliation is the point of forgiveness.

> . . . but God shows his love for us in that while we were still sinners, Christ died for us. . . . For if while we were enemies we were reconciled to God by the death of his Son, much more, now that we are reconciled, shall we be saved by his life. More than that, we also rejoice in God through our Lord Jesus Christ, through whom we have now received reconciliation.
>
> *(Rom. 5:8, 10–11)*

Reconciliation is also the point when we forgive one another. When someone confesses their sin against you and asks for your forgiveness, you don't forgive that person just to make yourself feel better, or even to make him or her feel better. The point of forgiveness is to remove the offense that has come between you, so that you can be reconciled to one another.

Forgiveness Is Not Consequence-Free

Of course, this commitment and reconciliation doesn't magically erase all of the consequences of sin. Many of those consequences will still have to be endured. My forgiveness of Nelson didn't instantly rebuild the trust that had been broken between us. That trust would need to be rebuilt over time. Your forgiveness of someone who carelessly dents the car you lent them doesn't automatically repair the damage. It still has to be paid for. But as you navigate the consequences of others' sin in your life, forgiveness provides the opportunity for that journey to be traveled *together*, as those who have been reconciled to one another just as God has reconciled us to himself.

Applying Forgiveness

What does all this mean for the times when you're sinned against by someone you're trying to help? As you minister to people in the midst of their mess, it's impossible to avoid being impacted by that mess yourself. Every person you care for, befriend, disciple, mentor, or counsel will be a sinner, and it will only be a matter of time before that person sins against you, sometimes significantly. Being sinned against hurts. It's discouraging, disappointing, disheartening, and betraying. But it's also an inevitable part of gospel care. That is why forgiveness must be an inevitable part of gospel care as well.

Without forgiveness, our attempts to help others become more like Christ will be short-lived. It won't take long before our relationships are broken by sin. And if we don't engage in God's path of reconciliation, our love for those we're ministering to will be cut short. So we should expect to be sinned against even by those we're striving so hard to love. We should expect to be hurt, slighted, and manipulated. The answer isn't to find the right boundaries or any other self-preservation technique. The answer to the difficulties we'll face in the process of ministering to fellow sinners is ultimately found in God's call to forgive.

But forgiveness isn't just a way to repair a relationship damaged by sin. Ultimately, our forgiveness of one another says even more about our understanding of God's forgiveness than it does anything else. This was the point Jesus made when he told the parable of the unforgiving servant:

> *Therefore the kingdom of heaven may be compared to a king who wished to settle accounts with his servants. When he began to settle, one was brought to him who owed him ten thousand talents. And since he could not pay, his master ordered him to be sold, with his wife and children and all that he had, and payment to be made. So the servant fell on his knees, imploring him, "Have patience with me, and I will pay you everything." And out of pity for him, the master of that servant released him and forgave him the debt. But when that same servant went out, he found one of his fellow servants who owed him a hundred denarii, and seizing him, he began to choke him, saying, "Pay what you owe." So his fellow servant fell down and pleaded with him, "Have patience with me, and I will pay you." He refused and went and put him in prison until he should pay the debt. When his fellow servants saw what had taken place, they were greatly distressed, and they went and reported to their master all that had taken place. Then his master summoned him and said to him, "You wicked servant! I forgave you all that debt because you pleaded with me. And should not you have had mercy on your fellow servant, as I had mercy on you?"*
>
> *(Matt. 18:23–33)*

As children of God who have been forgiven by God for more than we could ever imagine, we ought to be the most forgiving people in the world. The truth is, forgiveness isn't an option for us. It's not something we have the ability to hem and haw over. To be unforgiving is, like the servant in the parable, to be completely ungrateful for the forgiveness we have received.

Those you're ministering to will sin against you. Sometimes it will be small, and sometimes it will be big. But, regardless of the size or even the frequency (Matt. 18:21–22), forgiving them is a fundamental part of God's call to love them just as he, through Christ, has loved you.

WHEN FORGIVENESS ISN'T AN OPTION

This discussion about forgiveness may have raised a lot of questions, and the scope of this chapter can't get to all of them.[7] But there is one question that seems important to address before we move on: What if the person you're ministering to is unrepentant and won't ask for forgiveness? What do you do when forgiveness isn't an option?

Unfortunately, this is a very realistic scenario. Messy people don't always want to get out of their mess. And sometimes they refuse to believe that they're even in a mess at all. Thankfully, Scripture doesn't leave us wondering but gives us specific instructions about what to do when this happens:

> *If your brother sins against you, go and tell him his fault, between you and him alone. If he listens to you, you have gained your brother. But if he does not listen, take one or two others along with you, that every charge may be established by the evidence of two or three witnesses. If he refuses to listen to them, tell it to the church. And if he refuses to listen even to the church, let him be to you as a Gentile and a tax collector.*
>
> *(Matt. 18:15–17)*

Many Christians call this applying the principle of "church discipline." But I'm not sure that's the most helpful, or even accurate, characterization of what Jesus is saying here. While the passage does involve a kind of consequence, or at least a commonsense recognition, for the unrepentant person, "discipline" isn't the theme that sticks out to me.

It seems more accurate to call this the principle of "loving pursuit." Just like we saw in the last chapter, pursuing someone is a natural outflow of genuine love. So when someone you love sins against you, you pursue them and tell them about their sin. In my own life and ministry, I've often found this to involve a series of conversations. This isn't a simple announcement of the other person's sin; it's engaging in an ongoing discussion as you patiently try to help the person understand the sin he or she has committed (which we'll talk more about in chapter 10).

If they're not repentant, you don't just give up and walk away. You continue to pursue. You bring along one or two other brothers or sisters in Christ who love them as well, and together try to patiently and graciously help them understand the reality and depth of their sin. If the person *still* remains unrepentant, you *still* pursue! You talk to the pastors of your local church so that the church as a whole may call them to repentance and plead with them to recognize the magnitude and significance of their sin. Ultimately, if the person is still unrepentant even in the face of the calls of their entire spiritual family, the final recognition isn't so much an act of "discipline" as a commonsense recognition of their spiritual state. The church is called to treat the person as someone who is unrepentant of their sin because . . . they are unrepentant of their sin.

This is why gospel care works best in the context of the local church. If you're ministering to others as a part of a parachurch ministry or an independent counseling center, or you're trying to live the Christian life apart from the local church, you have nowhere to go when things get *really* messy. This is what God has designed the local church for. He has given the church identifiable membership and loving shepherds and built a supportive spiritual family for just this reason.

But even the "final" stage of the process Jesus describes above doesn't mean that our pursuit should end. Letting someone be like a "Gentile and a tax collector" isn't the end of the road. What did Jesus do to Gentiles and tax collectors? He pursued them!

There are many different ways we can love those we're ministering to, even when they're unrepentant. And we do so in the hope that, eventually, we'll be able to be reconciled to them through forgiveness as well. "Let all bitterness and wrath and anger and clamor and slander be put away from you, along with all malice. Be kind to one another, tenderhearted, forgiving one another, as God in Christ forgave you" (Eph. 4:31–32).

This kind of Christlike love shows its genuineness through practical, sacrificial service. When bitterness and anger have been replaced with tenderness and grace, they lead us to pray consistently, pursue intentionally, share generously, bear patiently, and forgive graciously.

But love that only listens and serves still hasn't fulfilled its God-given design. For love to be genuine, it also has to open its mouth and speak.

Endnotes

1. Klyne Snodgrass, *Ephesians, NIV Application Commentary*, 197.
2. John Calvin, *Calvin's Commentaries*, Vol. 21, 267.
3. Chris Brauns, *Unpacking Forgiveness*, 51.
4. Brauns, *Unpacking Forgiveness*, 51.
5. Ken Sande, *The Peacemaker*, 206.
6. Sande, *Peacemaker*, 209.
7. There are several good resources available for further study on the topic of forgiveness: Brauns, *Unpacking Forgiveness*; Sande, *Peacemaker*; Robert D. Jones, *Pursuing Peace*.

CHAPTER 9

STRENGTH FOR TODAY AND BRIGHT HOPE FOR TOMORROW

Speaking, Part 1

Claudia and her husband, Jorge, are good friends of ours. They are also leaders in our church and the type of couple that regularly engages in gospel care. They spend much of their free time discipling friends, community group members, and even a few high school students they have connected with. God has used them repeatedly in other people's lives, and they truly live out the kind of ministry this book describes. But being used by God in the midst of other people's messes doesn't mean you don't have messes of your own.

Claudia had a rough childhood but met Jorge relatively early in life, and they have been best friends ever since. She has a beautiful family, great friends, a loving husband, financial security, and a magnetic personality. But she has also been plagued by chronic depression. Claudia had been on the roller coaster of depression for years and tried every conceivable way to get off, but to no avail. As a result, she doubted God's goodness on a regular basis and turned to food as her "go-to" coping mechanism. Whether her views of God and food had caused her depression or resulted from it was impossible to determine. At this point it was all one big, tangled mess.

When I stopped by their apartment on the way home from the office one day, Claudia did me the honor of entrusting me with some of her darkest and most discouraging thoughts. Jorge had invited me over because they were at a particularly low point, and it felt like the roller coaster had dipped into a tunnel without a glimmer of light ahead.

I listened and asked questions while Claudia confessed the lies that had grabbed ahold of her mind. There were lies about God's identity, lies about her identity, lies about her guilt, and lies about her shame. They all came spilling out and her cold, hardened demeanor communicated that she was on the verge of giving up. But the most devastating lie of all was the one she kept repeating over and over: "I've tried everything." It was the voice of hopelessness.

In addition to patiently listening, I had spent the drive over praying for Claudia, and I bore with her as her accusations against God morphed into accusations against me and the church. But loving Claudia required more than just knowing and serving her. Love required that I speak.

Claudia needed more than just compassion and understanding. She needed truth to combat the lies that had filled her heart and mind. She needed biblical reminders that could cut through the despondency and show her that hope was real and that God was at work. As I considered what was most needed in that moment, it became very obvious that I needed to speak. While there wasn't a quick fix available, I knew that the long path forward was paved with words.

Speaking in Love

As we've seen in the last few chapters, gospel care is more than speaking words, but it isn't less. Words are the most powerful resource in the created universe. The universe itself came into being through words (Gen. 1:3–25). Words are the means by which God chose to communicate with us and relate to us, both in his Son (John 1:14) and in Scripture (2 Tim. 3:16). And words are the primary means we have to relate to one another. They are the building blocks of our intelligence and the key that unlocks our transformation (Heb. 4:12). So we can't possibly love one another well in the midst of the mess without using the most powerful tool at our disposal: words.

The power of words can be used for both good and bad. When used for good, words are *really* good. When used for bad, words are *really* bad. Solomon captures this in one of my favorite Proverbs:

There is one whose rash words are like sword thrusts,
but the tongue of the wise brings healing.

(Prov. 12:18)

Words have the power to wound like a stab in the back. But they also have the power to heal. Think about that for a second. You possess within your heart and mind something that, when offered in love, has the power to bring healing. How much would you have to hate someone to withhold such an amazing gift? As we read elsewhere in Proverbs,

Oil and perfume make the heart glad,
and the sweetness of a friend comes from his
earnest counsel.

(Prov. 27:9)

While listening to someone and practically serving them will bless them in innumerable ways, the sweetness of gospel care comes from our speaking. This is what the author of Hebrews insists should be taking place every single day in the life of every Christian: "Take care, brothers, lest there be in any of you an evil, unbelieving heart, leading you to fall away from the living God. But exhort one another every day, as long as it is called 'today,' that none of you may be hardened by the deceitfulness of sin" (Heb. 3:12–13). The word translated "exhort" here contains a cornucopia of connotations. It means to warn, to correct, to encourage, and to comfort.[1] As we'll see in this chapter and the next, there are all kinds of different words that are involved in gospel care. But the first thing to recognize is the biblical author's expectation that this kind of speech will be taking place each and every day. If you wake up and the day ends in "y," it's a day to speak truth to those around you.

It makes me think of a silly game my kids like to play whenever there's a balloon in our house. They try to see how long they can keep the balloon off the ground without catching it. Sometimes they use big hits that send the balloon up to the ceiling. Sometimes they use more frequent small taps that allow them more control.

In order to not succumb to the gravity of sin and its deceitfulness in our fallen world, we similarly need constant reminders of truth that lift us back up. We need big hits like Sunday mornings, but we also need little daily taps that come in the form of text messages, discipleship meetings, or conversations over coffee. This is how God has designed for us to grow. It is how we build one another up. *This* is how we become more like him.

> [S]peaking the truth in love, we are to grow up in
> every way into him who is the head, into Christ,
> from whom the whole body, joined and held
> together by every joint with which it is equipped,
> when each part is working properly, makes the
> body grow so that it builds itself up in love,
>
> (Eph. 4:15–16)

As I mentioned in chapter 1, truth and love are *both* required for genuine gospel care. Truth and love are like hydrogen and oxygen to someone dying of thirst. Alone they're useless. A canister filled with oxygen doesn't do the dying man any good. A canister filled with hydrogen is similarly worthless. But when combined together they become the life-giving substance (H_2O) that is so desperately needed.[2] Apart they offer nothing. Together they offer everything—just like truth and love.

We've already talked a lot about the essential nature of love. In the remainder of the book we're going to explore the kind of truth that we are called to speak as a manifestation of that love. It's not enough that we simply speak with those we're ministering to (even if we speak to them every day); the words we speak need to be true. In the midst of their messes, people need more than our opinions or our observations. They need truth.

Our world has developed all sorts of different ideas about the nature of truth, often questioning its very existence. But people need truth. We see this in our world, and we know it in our hearts. The further we drift from truth, the more doubt, confusion, and falsehoods reign, and our lives get messier and messier. We also need more than an ambiguous definition of truth. I need more than "my truth" and you need more than "your truth." What we need is *the* truth. So we must turn to the place where God, in his perfect wisdom, has chosen to reveal the truth to us: his Word.

> *All Scripture is breathed out by God and profitable*
> *for teaching, for reproof, for correction, and for*
> *training in righteousness, that the man of God may*
> *be complete, equipped for every good work.*
> *(2 Tim. 3:16–17)*

Not only has Scripture been breathed out by God, but it contains the only truth that genuinely transforms. If the goal of our ministry is to help one another become more like Christ, we need the Word of Christ to show us the way. We should be just as discontent with counsel that is not rooted in the Word of God as we are with a sermon that is not rooted in the Word of God. If a preacher spends Sunday mornings offering his own thoughts and not God's thoughts, he's lost sight of the calling he's been given by God. And when you and I (as we so often do) spend our deep conversations with one another simply swapping our own ideas, we've similarly lost sight of our calling as well.

In his Great Commission, Jesus calls us to make disciples not by teaching people everything *we* think is good or helpful, but by teaching them everything *he* taught his disciples:

> *And Jesus came and said to them, "All authority*
> *in heaven and on earth has been given to me.*
> *Go therefore and make disciples of all nations,*
> *baptizing them in the name of the Father and of the*
> *Son and of the Holy Spirit, teaching them to observe*
> *all that I have commanded you. And behold, I am*
> *with you always, to the end of the age."*
> *(Matt. 28:18–20)*

When we look through the Gospels at not only *what* Jesus taught his disciples but also *how* he taught them, we see the perfect example of what I've been calling gospel care. While there are many instances of Jesus' public ministry to crowds, the Gospels paint a picture of his much more intimate ministry as well. He regularly ministered to individuals and small groups of disciples around dinner tables, at weddings, on hills, and along the road. Whether it was Nicodemus late at night (John 3), a Samaritan woman at a well (John 4), Martha at a funeral (John 11), or his disciples during the Passover (John 13–14), Jesus was always speaking the truth in love.

Nicodemus was in the mess of religiosity, searching for reality; Jesus told him the truth that he must be born again. The Samaritan woman was in the mess of her adulterous life, thirsty for something that would satisfy; Jesus told her the truth that she could have living water. Martha was in the mess of her brother's death, looking for someone to blame; Jesus told her the truth about eternal life. The disciples were entering into the mess of their plans and dreams being shattered; Jesus told them the truth about a greater plan and a greater dream.

Each moment required truth. But each moment required different specific truths. And this is exactly what we're called to as we engage in gospel care. Each different mess will require truth. Not theories, not opinions; truth. But each mess will require different truths in subtly different forms. As we will explore in this chapter and the next, some will require *teaching*, some will require *correction*, and some will require *affirmation*. But *all* will require *hope*.

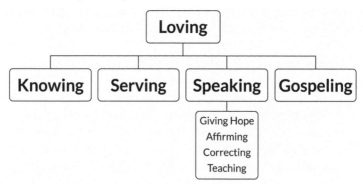

How and when we give hope, affirm, correct, or teach will inevitably be directed by wisdom as we consider what is most needed in each specific moment. But these ought to be familiar notes, played skillfully and played often. Ministering to others without these notes would be like trying to play a jazz solo in B-flat without using C, E-flat, or F. It would ruin the song. But when they're included, these centrally important notes allow the power and beauty of the song to come to life.

GIVING HOPE

So, in speaking the truth, where do we begin? While every person's mess is unique and there are no two situations you will come across that are the same, there is one common temptation I find in every situation I've come across: hopelessness. Whether the mess comes in the form of addiction, depression, guilt, marital struggles, discrimination, abuse, or fear, the temptation to hopelessness is always a part of the cocktail. This is why giving hope must always be a part of gospel care.

You hear hopelessness in phrases like "I can't" or "I've tried everything." It's behind explanations like "My roommates *make me* angry" or "My boss *makes me* anxious." It's at the root of the cry, "If only I had _____!"

I've yet to find an exception. People who have been in a mess for a long time need hope, and people who have just entered into a mess need hope. People who are making big decisions need hope, and people who are making small decisions need hope. People who are suffering need hope, and people who are in sin need hope. People who are young need hope, and people who are old need hope. Every person in every situation imaginable needs hope.

This is why Scripture is so saturated with it. Our souls need reminders of hope each and every day. We need reminders from others, and we need to remind ourselves. As the psalmist exhorted his own soul:

> *For God alone, O my soul, wait in silence,*
> *for my hope is from him.*
>
> *(Ps. 62:5)*

The problem is that we all tend to look for our hope in things other than God. We look for hope in our careers, our financial plans, our families, or our own ingenuity and strength. Even as we seek to provide gospel care, we can fall into the trap of pointing people to false hopes. While we may easily identify the obvious false hopes that plague people's hearts, we may simultaneously encourage them to put their hope in more subtle false hopes like our counsel, their pastors, or even the promise of having "more faith." People don't need us to tell them to have more faith. They need us to give them more hope.

To the extent that we encourage others to put hope in *anything* other than God himself, we will ultimately be feeding their hopelessness. To the extent that we help others put their hope in God, we will be feeding the flames of their desire for him. But to do so, the flame of hope must be burning in us as well. When people are hopeless, they invite us into their hopelessness. "I've tried everything" isn't just an opinion; it's the statement of an alleged fact. The temptation is for you, as a friend, discipler, or counselor, to believe it. If it's true that this person has tried everything, then you don't really have anything to offer, do you?

Giving hope begins with having hope. As the author of Hebrews declares so fervently, "Let us hold fast the confession of our hope without wavering, for he who promised is faithful" (Heb. 10:23). He knows that our holding fast to hope naturally results in our giving that hope to others. We can't share what we don't have. But whatever we have, we can't help but share. The writer continues, "And let us consider how to stir up one another to love and good works, not neglecting to meet together, as is the habit of some, but encouraging one another, and all the more as you see the Day drawing near" (Heb. 10:24–25).

But what exactly is our hope? Does Scripture give us hope that the mess will go away? Does it teach us that if we do the right things and act the right way, we'll be able to climb up out of the mess? Does it show us the easy way out?

Wayne Mack provides an excellent definition of what true biblical hope is: "True hope is a biblically based expectation of good . . . an expectation based on the promises of God."[3] In the midst of the mess, in the midst of the struggle and the pain, hope is the reminder that God is real, that transformation is possible, and that the best is yet to come. Let's look at how we can know this is true from the pages of Scripture.

HOPE IN LIGHT OF GOD'S PAST GRACE

The center of our hope is found in God's past grace for us through the Son. You'll often find that people need reminders of basic gospel truths not only to motivate heart transformation (as we'll explore in chapter 13) but just to have hope at all. Feelings of guilt and shame can be some of the most significant barriers to someone hearing *anything* you're saying. So you may need to start with simply reminding them of truths like those found at the beginning of Romans 8:

> *There is therefore now no condemnation for those who are in Christ Jesus. For the law of the Spirit of life has set you free in Christ Jesus from the law of sin and death. For God has done what the law, weakened by the flesh, could not do. By sending his own Son in the likeness of sinful flesh and for sin, he condemned sin in the flesh, in order that the righteous requirement of the law might be fulfilled in us, who walk not according to the flesh but according to the Spirit.*
>
> *(Rom. 8:1–4)*

"There is . . . no condemnation for those who are in Christ Jesus." Jesus has completed the work. It is done. It is finished. Past grace cuts through the guilt and shame that so regularly plague our hearts and delivers the medicine right to the source. "Past grace gives you the ability to fearlessly see yourself in the mirror of God's gaze, and gives you a reason to become different."[4] Past grace gives you a reason to hope.

HOPE IN LIGHT OF GOD'S PRESENT GRACE

God's grace isn't only a thing of the past. We also find hope in God's present grace through the Spirit. Earlier in his letter to the Romans, Paul makes a connection between the past work of Christ and our present transformation. God has not saved us, forgiven us, and reconciled us, only to then leave us alone; now he is transforming us into the image of his Son. And, as we will explore in future chapters, he's not only transforming us in the mess of our sin, but he's transforming us in the mess of our suffering as well:

> *Therefore, since we have been justified by faith, we have peace with God through our Lord Jesus Christ. Through him we have also obtained access by faith into this grace in which we stand, and we rejoice in hope of the glory of God. Not only that, but we rejoice in our sufferings, knowing that*

*suffering produces endurance, and endurance
produces character, and character produces hope,
and hope does not put us to shame, because
God's love has been poured into our hearts
through the Holy Spirit who has been given to us.*

(Rom. 5:1–5)

Notice the final link in this chain of transformation: hope. God promises to redeem our suffering by using it to produce in us strength and endurance. And he promises to use that endurance to bring about a true heart change: character. And he promises that this character will give us hope because we will see with our own eyes and by our own experience that God is real and that he truly is working in our lives. Present grace in the midst of our sufferings gives us reason to hope.

There is reason for hope not only in our suffering, but also in the midst of our sin. Our sin is not odd or even unique. In fact, our sin is a part of the common experience of being human in this fallen world. As a result, we are not too bad, too troubled, or too far gone to be transformed. In fact, we are perfectly normal: we're sinners. And as sinners our lives are constantly plagued by various temptations. God knows this and promises to provide us with everything we need to grow and change, even in the face of the most seemingly overwhelming temptations:

"No temptation has overtaken you that is not common to man. God is faithful, and he will not let you be tempted beyond your ability, but with the temptation he will also provide the way of escape, that you may be able to endure it" (1 Cor. 10:13).

On top of this, God promises to empower us to endure temptation. He calls us his workmanship, he tells us that he has already prepared our good works beforehand, and he promises that he will bring his work in us to completion. All acts of his grace!

*For by grace you have been saved through faith. And
this is not your own doing; it is the gift of God, not a
result of works, so that no one may boast. For we are his
workmanship, created in Christ Jesus for good works,
which God prepared beforehand, that we should walk
in them.*

(Eph. 2:8–10)

And I am sure of this, that he who began a good work in
you will bring it to completion at the day of Jesus Christ.
(Phil. 1:6)

Present grace in the midst of your sin gives you reason to hope.

HOPE IN LIGHT OF GOD'S FUTURE GRACE

God's promises assure us that his grace will also extend far into the future. As a result, we can have hope because of the Father's promise of future grace.

First, God's promises give us reason to hope for the future of our lives here on earth. He promises that, not only will he redeem what we have experienced, he will also redeem whatever lies ahead: "And we know that for those who love God all things work together for good, for those who are called according to his purpose. For those whom he foreknew he also predestined to be conformed to the image of his Son, in order that he might be the firstborn among many brothers" (Rom. 8:28–29). God promises that, in his mysterious sovereignty, he will redeem everything that happens to us by using it for our ultimate good. He also reminds us what our ultimate good is: "to be conformed to the image of his Son." God promises that he will use everything that happens to us in our lives to bring about the goal we've been talking about all along: Christlikeness. What a promise!

But his future grace doesn't stop there. His grace isn't only for redemption in this life, but also for the promise of the life to come. Paul continues by pointing out in the very next verse that God's sovereign work will result in our ultimate glorification:

And those whom he predestined he also called,
and those whom he called he also justified, and
those whom he justified he also glorified.
(Rom. 8:30)

Glorification may not be a concept you spend much time thinking about, but it's one that can offer incredible hope. In his first letter to the Thessalonians, Paul paints a picture of what this glorification is going to be like, and it's helpful for us to read and imagine.

Picture this:

> *For this we declare to you by a word from the*
> *Lord, that we who are alive, who are left until*
> *the coming of the Lord, will not precede those*
> *who have fallen asleep. For the Lord himself will*
> *descend from heaven with a cry of command,*
> *with the voice of an archangel, and with the*
> *sound of the trumpet of God. And the dead in*
> *Christ will rise first. Then we who are alive, who*
> *are left, will be caught up together with them in*
> *the clouds to meet the Lord in the air, and so we*
> *will always be with the Lord. Therefore encourage*
> *one another with these words.*
>
> *(1 Thess. 4:15–18)*

Don't miss the impact of that last sentence. I'm afraid that most people reading this passage think of it simply as an "eschatology" (the study of the end times) passage. They parse it out, looking for certain interpretive clues that will inform their theological stances on the how, when, and where of Christ's return. But verse 18 reveals to us that Paul's main point in writing this was so that his readers might be encouraged. "We will always be with the Lord." What an incredible reason for hope! This passage wasn't written for the purpose of speculative theology, it was written for gospel care.

As we sat together on their small apartment patio and I listened to Claudia share her heart, the words of 1 Thessalonians 5:14 ran through my head: "And we urge you, brothers, admonish the idle, encourage the fainthearted, help the weak, be patient with them all." Claudia was obviously in need of encouragement. She wasn't idle, and she wasn't even particularly weak; but her hopelessness had left her utterly fainthearted.

There were lots of truths that Claudia would need to hear over the coming weeks, months, and even years. There were lots of things that needed to be said, and there would be time to say them. But before she would be able to hear anything else, Claudia needed to hear that there was hope. Maybe she didn't believe it yet, but she needed to hear that I still believed it. I had listened to everything she had said, and I still believed that God's promises to her were true. I still believed there was hope.

ENDNOTES

1. Peter T. O'Brien, *The Letter to the Hebrews*, 147–148.
2. Yes, science nerds, I'm aware that they could also combine to form hydrogen peroxide . . . but just go with me.
3. Wayne Mack, *Counseling: How to Counsel Biblically*, 118.
4. David Powlison, *Speaking the Truth in Love*, 42.

CHAPTER 10

MORE THAN A FRIEND

Speaking, Part 2

A s the parents of four kids, Lara and I have realized that we have a lot to learn about people, how they're motivated, and how to help them. Gospel care with adults is one thing, but trying to help our young kids in the midst of their messes is a whole other ballgame. Each one of our kids is unique. They all have very different personalities and are motivated by different things. Sometimes we feel like we've got a handle on things and we understand each of them pretty well. Other times it feels like we're headed down a hill at 100 mph and the wheels are coming off.

One night we found ourselves in the midst of one of these "wheels coming off" moments, not knowing what to do. In addition to all of our kids experiencing new challenges, we had been having a particularly tough time with one of them. His attitude felt out of control. His defiance seemed to be getting worse and worse. His tantrums would undo the whole house. And we felt stuck. As those who often offer the truth and love of gospel care to those around us, it had become apparent that this was one of the moments when we were in desperate need of help ourselves.

So we called a friend, Theresa, whose kids were a few years older than ours and whose life and parenting we knew well and respected, and we asked if she would come over to talk. As we all sat down in our family room, I began to explain the situation and Lara described what we had tried and how nothing seemed to be working. We felt helpless. We felt defeated. We felt hopeless. Theresa listened carefully and asked a few questions about the details of the situation. And I waited, fairly impatiently, for her to speak.

I knew enough to *know* there were things we were missing. I was prepared for the correction that would be coming and, in fact, was excited for it. I couldn't wait to find out what we had been doing wrong so that we could fix it and get our son back on the right track. Even if it hurt, even if there were issues I had to deal with that hadn't come up before, I was prepared for it. We had prayed about our desire to have open hearts to whatever Theresa would tell us, and I was ready.

What I wasn't ready for was what Theresa actually said. Theresa simply affirmed us. Now, it's not that we were being perfect parents; far from it. But Theresa wisely knew that, in that moment, what we wanted was something different from what we actually needed. We were looking for the adjustment that would supercharge our parenting. But Theresa knew that the path forward for us as parents wasn't to find a new solution or even to change much of what we were doing. It was to continue to patiently and faithfully pray, discipline, love, explain, correct, and enjoy our son, just as we had been doing. Theresa knew that the words that were most needed at *that* moment were words of biblical affirmation.

Affirming

Biblical affirmation isn't what usually comes to mind when we think of speaking the truth in love. We tend to think of correction, teaching, exhortation, or rebuke. If someone is headed in the right direction, why would they need truth spoken to them? If they're already on the right path, what is there to say? But Scripture models for us (and personal experience confirms) that affirmation is a powerful tool in helping others become more like Jesus.

I believe one of the main reasons affirmation gets a bad rap is because our culture has come to affirm *everything*, whether it's true or not. We tell *every* kid that they were great on the baseball field. We tell *every* employee that they're vital to the company. We tell *every* fan in the stands that they were instrumental to their team winning the game. The problem is that the kid, the employee, and the fan all know when it's not actually true. Biblical affirmation is not saying nice things to build someone's self-esteem. Biblical affirmation is the recognition of gifts, strengths, and growth in a person's life in order to promote God esteem.

Affirmation is not one of those things that comes naturally to me. I'm not sure it comes naturally to many of us. In fact, my co-pastors used to joke that my highest form of praise around the office was when I would say, "You know, that's not a horrible idea."

But a turning point in my life happened when I picked up Sam Crabtree's incredible book *Practicing Affirmation* (or maybe one of the other pastors put it on my desk). In it I found myself confronted by the fact that, when I fail to regularly affirm others, I'm not only withholding love from them, I'm also withholding praise from God. I was neglecting a powerful tool God had given me to bless others and to glorify him. "We rob God of praise by not pointing out his reflection in the people he has knit together in his image. . . . God-centered affirmations point toward the echoes, shadows, and reality of a righteousness not intrinsic to the person being affirmed."[1]

The point of biblical affirmation is to recognize the unnatural, otherwise impossible, presence of Christlikeness in another person. When someone becomes more like Jesus, it is a Spirit-empowered miracle that ought to be recognized and celebrated. Christlikeness is the object of affirmation. And if Christlikeness is *also* the goal of gospel care, as we've discussed, then we should regularly be looking for evidence of it in the lives of those we're ministering to so we can point it out and encourage them onward.

In his most encouraging, affirmation-filled letter, Paul exemplifies this as he exhorts and encourages the Thessalonians. He repeatedly affirms the work God is doing in them and encourages them to continue on in the same direction "more and more":

> *Finally, then, brothers, we ask and urge you in the Lord Jesus, that as you received from us how you ought to walk and to please God, just as you are doing, that you do so more and more.*
>
> *(1 Thess. 4:1)*

> *For God has not destined us for wrath, but to obtain*
> *salvation through our Lord Jesus Christ, who died for*
> *us so that whether we are awake or asleep we might*
> *live with him. Therefore encourage one another and*
> *build one another up, just as you are doing.*
>
> *(1 Thess. 5:9–11)*

Sometimes our journey to become more like Jesus doesn't require correction or turning in a different direction. Sometimes it simply requires continuing on in the direction we're already headed. In fact, as we minister to people who are truly being transformed, we should expect that to be the case.

As we see the budding fruit of the Spirit appear in a person's life, we should help them see it too. We should be "fruit-spotters" on the lookout for love, joy, peace, and patience just like an excited wildlife watcher who finally sees that elk, bear, or moose he has been looking for. There's kindness! There's goodness! I see self-control! I've never met a wildlife watcher who was content to leave the discovery to himself. He wants others to know what he's seen. That's exactly what we're doing in biblical affirmation: pointing out what we've seen for the glory of God and the good of the person we've seen it in.

Crabtree identifies four characteristics of good affirmation that I've found particularly helpful over the years.[2] First, as we've talked about, good affirmation is always God-centered. It is praise for what *God* has done in the life of the affirmed. Second, good affirmation is always honest. Again, biblical affirmation isn't about falsely propping up people's views of themselves. It doesn't involve flattery or exaggeration, but reflects an honest recognition of the incredible work God has done in a person's life.

Third, and possibly most challenging for those of us who have yet to make this a habit, good affirmation is always steady. In other words, it's a regular, common part of life. Too often, affirmation becomes the exception instead of the rule. There are many things that should be a part of your daily routine: brushing your teeth, taking a shower, reading your Bible, and affirming those around you. Affirmation is fundamental to the Christian life. It's an important part of the "exhorting one another" we are called to do "every day, as long as it is called 'today'" (Heb. 3:13).

Finally, good affirmation ought to be detached from correction. This may be a new idea even for the most ardent affirmers. It seems like most of us have been taught that the best way to offer criticism is to do so as part of an affirmation sandwich: something-good/something-bad/something-good. But when affirmations are used to cushion the blow of criticism or critique, they lose much of their God-glorifying, gospel-motivating power. While we're going to talk about correction in the next section, it's important to recognize that affirmation isn't just the nicety required to prepare a person for correction. Affirmation is a significant act of love, in and of itself. And sometimes it's all that's needed to propel others forward on their journey of becoming more like Christ.

CORRECTING

While the words I needed to hear that night from Theresa were words of affirmation, there have been many times I've needed to hear something else. I think of the time when one of my closest friends knew that he should question the way I was speaking to my wife, regardless of the fact that he wasn't married himself. Or the time a co-pastor helped me see that my thoughts about other church leaders were not only unloving, but untrue and divisive. Or the time one of my children pointed out that my cell phone habits were inconsistent with both the Bible and even my own teaching on the subject (OK . . . the last one has happened a few different times). There have been countless moments in my life when what was most needed was a kind and gentle correction, and there will be countless times when that is exactly what people in your life need as well.

Correcting one another can be scary. It's not something most of us enjoy doing. It can feel like we're putting our relationship at risk by pointing out how another person's behavior or thoughts or emotions are not consistent with the call of Christ. So we tend to simply go along, looking the other way, trying to maintain the peace. But looking the other way is not what Jesus had in mind when he instructed his disciples to turn the other cheek. There's no love in looking the other way.

It's not loving to let your roommate walk out the door on a date with a big piece of spinach in her teeth. It's not loving for a father to let his child write all his letters backwards. It's not loving for a doctor to tell her patient to eat whatever he wants regardless of how it's contributing to his illness. And it's not loving for you to fail to correct someone when you see sin in their life. Correction is loving. As David Mathis writes, "One of the most loving things we can do for each other in the church is tell each other when we're wrong."[3]

Genuine love requires speaking words of correction. But I'm afraid that one of the main reasons we're so apprehensive about offering correction is because we've so rarely seen it connected to genuine love. Correction without love is cold, harsh, judgmental, and often cruel. We've all experienced this kind of correction before, and it hurts.

Correction without love comes from seeing ourselves as somehow different from those we're correcting. We stand with God in judgment of the pitiful sinner standing in front of us. It makes me think of Dwight Schrute, the character from *The Office*, who repeatedly stands next to his manager, Michael Scott, introducing himself as the "Assistant Regional Manager," only to be corrected because he is, in fact, the "Assistant *to the* Regional Manager." You and I are not "Assistant Gods." We are simply assistants *to* the one true God. Our correct place is not next to God looking down in judgment on sinners. We belong standing side by side with our fellow sinners before a perfectly righteous and overwhelmingly gracious God.

As we stand side by side with one another, correction takes on a very different tone. We stand as fellow sinners similarly in need of correction and familiar with God's amazing grace. We stand as fellow sinners who have taken the time to remove the logs out of our own eyes before beginning to help our neighbors with the specks in theirs (Matt. 7:3–5). We correct, not out of self-righteousness or self-importance, but out of brotherly love.

Just think about the power and beauty of correction when it comes from someone who has taken the time to truly know you, has sacrificed for you, and has given you genuine biblical hope. In the context of this kind of relationship, you would welcome the gentle tap of correction because it would inevitably be delivered with compassion and care. In fact, it's this love-inspired gentleness that is one of the hallmarks of Christian correction:

Brothers, if anyone is caught in any
transgression, you who are spiritual should
restore him in a spirit of gentleness . . .

(Gal. 6:1)

And the Lord's servant must not be quarrelsome
but kind to everyone, able to teach, patiently
enduring evil, correcting his opponents with
gentleness. God may perhaps grant them
repentance leading to a knowledge of the truth.

(2 Tim. 2:24–25)

Unfortunately, many of us are so unfamiliar with loving correction that we have a hard time even imagining what it looks like. But, just like the other forms of speech, loving correction comes in different forms depending on what's most needed.

Sometimes correction can come in the form of an illustration. Think of Nathan correcting David by telling a fictional story about a rich man who stole a poor man's lamb in order to feed his guest (2 Sam. 12:1–7). David became furious and was quickly able to see the injustice in the fictional story. The illustration prepared him to see the similar injustice in his own actions.

Sometimes correction can come in the form of a story from your own life. Maybe you have fallen short in similar ways and sharing your own struggles can light the path for another person to travel. Be careful, though, because we can also project our motives onto others, sometimes indicting them in ways that we might deserve, but they do not. This is why I tend to offer this kind of correction as an idea to share instead of a conclusion to announce. When you invite someone to consider whether they may have similar sinful motives to yours, you allow them space to consider the reality of their own heart.

It can also be helpful to offer correction in the form of prompting questions. Invite your friend to correct himself. More often than not he'll get there more quickly than you think. Ask general questions like, "How do you think God views that area of your life?" or "What would you tell me if our situations were reversed?" Ask specific questions like, "What else could you have said in that situation?" or "What do you think the Bible would call that emotion?" My experience is that patient, prompting questions will result in the correction that is needed the vast majority of the time.

At the same time, illustrations, stories, and questions won't facilitate the needed correction all the time. Sometimes you will need to offer a direct rebuke. When those you're ministering to don't have the biblical knowledge or spiritual openness to get there on their own, you will inevitably need to correct them gently, but firmly, and confidently. Jesus' direct corrections of his disciples provide excellent examples of what this looks like when done well. His kindness was matched by his firmness in moments like James and John's request to have privileged seats in heaven (Mark 10:35–40), the disciples' decision to keep children away from him (Mark 10:13–16), or Peter's refusal to let Jesus wash his feet (John 13:8). Firmness and gentleness are not mutually exclusive. Inevitably there will be times when what is most needed will be a firm and unambiguous rebuke. And, every once in a while, the situation may even require a good old-fashioned, "O foolish Galatians! Who has bewitched you?" (Gal. 3:1).

Don't underestimate the power and importance of correction, in any form, when offering gospel care. To correct someone who is wandering (or running) away from Christ is one of the kindest acts of love we can perform. Just as a surgeon cuts his patient for their ultimate good, you are called to correct for the sake of love.

> Better is open rebuke
> than hidden love.
> Faithful are the wounds of a friend.
>
> *(Prov. 27:5–6)*

TEACHING

Sometimes those you're ministering to will be on the right path and need to be affirmed. Sometimes they will have wandered off the path and need to be corrected. But sometimes they won't even know where the path is. This is why, in addition to affirmation and correction, teaching is such an important part of gospel care. A key component of discipleship is helping to teach others what they don't yet know. If you've been a Christian for any amount of time, you have been taught: you've been taught who God is, you've been taught what he has done, you've been taught how the world works, and you've been taught how you are called to live. As someone who has been taught so much, a significant part of your calling is to take what you've been given and teach it to others.

Just as Paul encouraged Timothy: "You then, my child, be strengthened by the grace that is in Christ Jesus, and what you have heard from me in the presence of many witnesses entrust to faithful men, who will be able to teach others also" (2 Tim. 2:1–2). And, as he makes clear to Titus, this call to teach isn't just a calling for men: "Older women likewise are to be reverent in behavior, not slanderers or slaves to much wine. They are to teach what is good" (Titus 2:3).

The vast majority of teaching in the local church takes place in the interpersonal relationships of gospel care. Far too many aspiring teachers or preachers long for the day when they can stand in front of a crowd and impart wisdom or exposit God's Word, but regularly neglect the countless opportunities they have every day to teach in interpersonal relationships. Everyone around you will inevitably require teaching. And that doesn't necessarily mean that they need to talk to a pastor, download a sermon, or read a book. In fact, much of the teaching they so desperately need should come from you. You are the one who knows them personally. You are the one who has taken the time to listen and understand their struggles. You are the one God is calling to teach.

While we could fill books and books (and many people have) describing all that we ought to be teaching one another, there are two overarching categories of teaching it is important to touch on. First, love seeks to teach practical wisdom that can help people in tangible and immediate ways. And, second, love seeks to teach theological truth that will address the deeper messes of our hearts.

TEACHING PRACTICAL WISDOM

At times, what is most needed in a particular moment is simply some practical wisdom. A couple may need to be taught to set aside fifteen minutes each night to talk with each other. A teen may need to be taught to install accountability software on his computer. A young professional may need to be taught how to use and follow a budget. An elderly woman may need to be taught how to use Uber or Lyft.

Scripture provides us with numerous examples of practical wisdom that doesn't necessarily get to a person's heart but is helpful for navigating life. In Proverbs we find practical wisdom about allowing people to suffer consequences (19:19), the outcome of diligent work (28:19), the foolishness of self-promotion (25:6–7), and even the benefit of a slow and steady investment strategy (13:11).

Even in the New Testament, we find an example of Paul (inspired by the Holy Spirit) offering practical wisdom to Timothy about the digestive problems he'd been having: "No longer drink only water, but use a little wine for the sake of your stomach and your frequent ailments" (1 Tim. 5:23). The Spirit's intention here was not to establish wine as the exclusive indigestion remedy for Christians. Paul was simply providing some practical advice for his good friend, and the Spirit was using it to give us an example of the loving nature of practical wisdom.

Oftentimes practical wisdom is just the relaying of common sense. But the thing about common sense is that it's not nearly as common as we would expect it to be. Common sense can seemingly desert even the most sober-minded of us, especially when we're in the chaos of life's messes. This is why offering practical wisdom can often be a compassionate fruit of love.

What practical wisdom or skills do you have that might help the person you're ministering to? Could he use help with managing the finances? Or what about her problem-solving skills? Does your friend need to work on time management? Would better sleep help him out? Could some basic communication skills go a long way? Or even a new workout routine? Is there some helpful form of technology she needs to learn how to navigate? Even if you yourself can't provide the practical wisdom your friend needs, don't forget you're part of a family! You're not engaged in gospel care as a lone ranger. There are many other brothers and sisters around you whose gifts or strengths might be a blessing to the person you're ministering to. Don't simply pass them off, but bring others into your relationship. Teaching practical wisdom can help remove significant barriers to spiritual growth.

TEACHING THEOLOGY

While practical wisdom can be helpful and incredibly loving, those we're ministering to will need more than tips and life hacks to become more like Jesus. The only way to become more like Jesus is to know him more. This is why we *must* teach theology to those we're ministering to as well.

Don't let me lose you here. "Theology" can be a pretty intimidating word. You may be saying to me (if you talk back to books like I do), "Look, Scott, I can spend time getting to know someone, I can serve them in practical ways, and I can even find some Bible verses to affirm or correct them as needed, but once you start talking about me teaching theology, you're way above my pay grade. We need to leave teaching theology to the professionals." If that's anywhere close to how you feel, I'm afraid you have an inaccurate definition of theology. So will you let me gently correct you?

"Theology" is a pretty simple word to take apart. You can probably do it on your own. *Theos* is the Greek word for God. And the *-logy* suffix, which also originated in Greek, has come to refer to "the study of" something. Theology is simply the study of God. Or, to put it a different way, theology is gaining the knowledge of God. If you know God at all, you know theology. The teaching of theology is simply the act of imparting what you know about God (who he is, what he's like, what he's done, what he's promised) to someone else.

And Scripture teaches us that it is theology (the knowledge of God) that truly transforms our hearts from the inside out. As we read in 2 Peter,

> *His divine power has granted to us all things*
> *that pertain to life and godliness, through the*
> *knowledge of him who called us to his own glory*
> *and excellence, by which he has granted to us his*
> *precious and very great promises, so that through*
> *them you may become partakers of the divine*
> *nature, having escaped from the corruption that*
> *is in the world because of sinful desire.*
>
> *(2 Peter 1:3–4)*

Everything we need for life and godliness (for becoming like Christ in the midst of the mess) has been given to us by God through theology (the knowledge of him). As one of my favorite seminary professors used to always tell us, "Theology is life." As we come to know God more and more in his "glory and excellence," and are taught and reminded of "his precious and very great promises," we increasingly become more and more like Christ as "partakers of [his] divine nature." We increasingly become those who have "escaped from the corruption that is in the world because of sinful desire." We become like Christ through knowing him. We become like Christ through theology.

This is why we will spend the final section of the book looking at the theology we are called to teach one another (and remind one another of) in the form of what I like to call "gospeling." Gospeling is the process of massaging the truth of God and the gospel into one another's hearts so that we might know him more accurately, love him more passionately, and follow him more diligently.

If we love those we're ministering to enough to want them to truly be transformed, we must do more than simply speak truth into their lives; we must point them to the Savior. We have to proclaim more than simply, "That was good" or "That was bad," or "This would be helpful" or "This will make you feel better." We must proclaim Christ.

> Him we proclaim, warning everyone and teaching
> everyone with all wisdom, that we may present
> everyone mature in Christ. For this I toil,
> struggling with all his energy that he powerfully
> works within me.
>
> (Col. 1:28–29)

Endnotes

1. Sam Crabtree, *Practicing Affirmation*, 18–19.
2. Crabtree, *Practicing Affirmation*, 64–71. List provided here in reverse order.
3. David Mathis, *Habits of Grace*, 185.

CHAPTER 11

THE *Mess* OUTSIDE OF US

Gospeling, Part 1

GOSPELING IN LOVE

This is where you're probably expecting to find another personal story, but I want to begin this chapter a little differently. The story's still coming, I promise, but before we get to it there's something important we need to discuss.

You see, I'm afraid this is the point in the book where you're going to be most tempted to stop reading. Because this is the point in our relationships where we tend to stop, too.

Think about that relationship that has been on your heart as you've read through the last ten chapters. Think about one of the names you wrote down back in chapter 7. If you've been seeking to genuinely love that person, that means you've taken the time to truly get to know them, listen to them, ask them questions, and consider what they really need. You've gone out of your way to sacrificially serve them, pray for them, and bear with them when things have gotten difficult. And you've graciously spoken words of truth to them: giving hope, affirming the areas of godly growth in their life, and correcting the areas of inconsistency. Sounds like a pretty successful relationship to me.

The problem is that a lot of us stop there. We look back on all of those manifestations of love and assume that is all that is needed. And we're not the only ones who are tempted to feel that way; the person you're ministering to might feel that way as well. No matter what kind of mess a person is struggling with, they will inevitably feel encouraged, strengthened, and spurred on if someone takes the time to know them, serve them, and speak truth to them. Most of the time, people assume that's all that personal ministry is.

However, remember what we talked about way back in chapter 2: the goal of all biblical personal ministry is Christlikeness. God wants to use you in other people's lives not just to make them feel better, not just to make them live more healthily, not just to give them a hand when they're in need, but ultimately to help them transform to become more like Christ. This is why the messy people in our lives need more than just our attention. They need the gospel.

We don't normally use the term "gospel" as a verb, but the New Testament (in its original language) repeatedly does. The angel Gabriel "gospeled" Zechariah when he announced the birth of John the Baptist (Luke 1:19). Philip "gospeled" the Ethiopian eunuch (Acts 8:35). Paul "gospeled" the Corinthians and then reminded them again of (literally) "the gospel I [gospeled] to you" (1 Cor. 15:1). And Jesus, along with his disciples, went throughout the cities and the villages "gospeling" about the kingdom of God (Luke 8:1).

Gospeling is essentially announcing the good news. But this announcement isn't just something we need before we know Christ; it's also a reminder we need every day as we walk with Christ. We not only need to be taught the gospel, we need to be constantly reminded of it as well. As Elyse Fitzpatrick and Denis Johnson write, "The truth of the gospel—that we are 'in' him— isn't meant only for those who are beginning the Christian life. It is meant for all of us *every day*."[1]

Reminders of gospel truth—who God is, who we are, who we are in Christ, what he has done for us, his future plans for us and for the world—are the fuel for our growth in Christlikeness. They are the Spirit-empowered means of the internal transformation we all long for as Christians.

But in order for the good news to make any sense, we first need eyes to see the reality of our world and our hearts. The gospel is only good news when we clearly understand the predicament we are in without it.

Jesus modeled this throughout his earthly ministry. It was the darkness of people's messes that made the news of the gospel so incredibly good. He met people in the depth of their suffering (Matt. 5:2–12; Mark 1:34) and he exposed the depth of their sin (Matt. 5:21–30; Luke 11:39–40). It was into this mess that he brought the message of eternal, abundant life (John 10:10).

He brought the promise of a new identity (John 1:12), of soul satisfaction (John 7:38–39), of lasting joy (John 16:20–24), and of unimaginable grace (John 3:16–17). And with this message came the inauguration of a new life. For those who would follow him, he had a radically different life in store. They would be called to take up their own crosses daily (Luke 9:23); they would be called to love others continually (John 13:34–35); they would be called to lay down their lives completely (John 15:12–14).

If we are to lovingly gospel our brothers and sisters in Christ, we will need to follow Christ's example. We'll need to help them look honestly at the depth of the mess they are in, and remind them of both the glorious hope they have in Christ and the radical life he is calling them to live. This is what we're going to unpack in this final section. We're going to look at the four distinct components that make up what it means to "gospel" someone:

○ *Recognizing* the impact of our fallen world (this chapter);

○ *Identifying* the depths of their fallen heart (ch. 12);

○ *Reminding* them of gospel truth (ch. 13);

○ *Instructing* them in gospel commands (ch. 14).

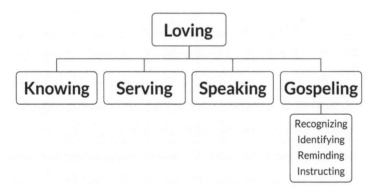

I hope this helps you catch a glimpse of why this final section is so incredibly important. Without gospeling, we're lacking the aspect of Christian love that gives everything else its ultimate meaning. Have you ever heard one of your favorite songs played with the lyrics removed? It's like listening to a karaoke track without anyone singing. That's what personal ministry is like without gospeling. It can be beautiful, it can be enjoyable, it can be moving, but without the lyrics it loses its ultimate purpose. A song that was written with lyrics was designed to convey something powerful and specific through those lyrics. To remove the lyrics is to remove that intended meaning. Similarly, gospel care without gospeling is missing the core of what it was intended to convey.

We will unpack each of the four components of gospeling in due time. But first, as I promised, let's get to that story.

It's been a long road for Arash and Leila. We've been friends for about seven years now, and it's difficult to recall if even one of the past seven years could be described as "easy." For a while we were in a community group together until the group got too big and we split into two. Arash and Leila led and hosted the new group, continually pouring themselves out for others even through some of the most difficult challenges of their lives.

Arash was Leila's second husband. Her first husband had died in a car crash only a couple of years into their marriage. Leila had thought she would never love again, that her heart simply couldn't take it. The grief was overwhelming and seemed to just drag on and on, long past when she had expected it to lift. But, after a few years, things slowly began to change, and at just the right moment God brought Arash into her life. Arash is a gentle and patient man with the heart of a servant. He opened Leila's heart in a way she thought had been closed forever.

Of course, navigating the emotional impact of a second marriage wasn't easy. But it seemed easy compared to everything that happened next. Arash and Leila's first child was a healthy, beautiful little girl named Sarah. Sarah was their joy and seemed to be the beginning of the fulfillment of all their dreams. As their little girl began to grow, however, they began to encounter challenges they hadn't expected. Sarah struggled with all kinds of sensory sensitivities and was easily overwhelmed when overstimulated. She found her emotions almost impossible to control and, in the coming years, every activity, every classroom, and every sports field would prove to be a new struggle. Eventually she was given a diagnosis on the autism spectrum.

Arash and Leila's second child, Jamie, came into their family through the foster system. Just like their daughter, he entered their family as a healthy, beautiful infant. But they soon began to see emotional and behavioral symptoms that were all too familiar. In God's perfect providence he had placed a second child with autistic struggles in their family. Now they would need to learn to navigate *two* therapists, *two* classroom aids, *two* individualized education plans, *two* circles of friends, and *two* kids with similar but very different struggles.

Two years later, Jamie's birth mom was pregnant again. She knew she couldn't keep the baby, but the one thing she wanted was for her children to be together, so the social worker asked Arash and Leila if there was room in their home for one more. While both Arash and Leila were being stretched thin, they couldn't imagine saying "no," and so, when he was born, little baby Benjamin entered their family as well.

One day, a couple of years later, I got a text from Leila to see if I could swing by their house on my way home from the office. Ben was now almost two years old and was well adjusted, a great sleeper, and a joy to have around. However, Ben wasn't the problem. Shortly after Ben had been born, Arash had lost his job. He was a highly skilled employee for a company that had gone bankrupt, and finding another position that suited his unique skill set had proved much harder than he had ever expected. They had burned through almost all of their retirement savings while Arash was looking for work. And now he was working in a position he was overqualified for, for a company with a horrific work culture that demanded long hours with almost no flexibility. As a result, Leila was essentially juggling life with their three kids all on her own.

Life wasn't only falling short of Arash and Leila's expectations, it was clearly falling short of the expectations of their extended families as well. Both being third-generation Americans, their families had strong cultures of financial success and upward mobility built on the sacrifices of their parents and grand-parents, but Arash and Leila were beginning to feel like they no longer fit into that narrative. The comments made by their parents weren't explicitly mean, but it was clear that this was not the life their parents had dreamed of for their children.

And now, on top of it all, Leila was pregnant again.

They reached out because they didn't know what to do. They reached out because they were teetering on the edge of hopelessness. So there I sat in their living room, just listening to Leila pour out her heart. She shared her fears, her frustrations, her guilt, and her doubts. But they didn't come out in those nice, neat categories; they came out like a waterfall of emotions all jumbled together.

Arash and Leila were in a mess. But what kind of mess were they in? There were definitely ways that their hearts were contributing to their mess. Their own expectations, desires, and selfish responses to their kids were absolutely a part of the problem. But their sin wasn't the *only* cause of the mess. There were significant external contributors to the mess as well.

Simply living in a fallen world was contributing to their mess in countless ways. The death of Leila's first husband was an external cause of the mess. The social struggles of their first two kids also made life messy. The choices of Jamie and Ben's birth mother, the broken school system that made getting classroom aides difficult, Arash's boss and the work culture at his company, and the expectations of their parents were all external causes of the mess; so were the hormonally induced struggles Leila was experiencing due to her pregnancy. All of these were contributing in significant ways to the mess Arash and Leila were in. This all left them wondering how the gospel applied when so much of the mess they found themselves in wasn't caused by their own personal sin.

OUR MISUNDERSTANDING OF SUFFERING

The world tends to overemphasize the impact of suffering on people's lives. Everyone is a victim of everything, and whatever mess you find yourself in is most likely your parents' fault, the culture's fault, your biology's fault, or the other political party's fault. Without the ability to call something "sin," the vast majority of the problems we face in life become someone else's fault.

I'm afraid, however, that in response to this culture of victimization, Christians have often swung the pendulum too far back the other way. As a result, large swaths of the church have unintentionally developed an overheated culture of personal responsibility. While the world sees suffering around every corner, the church can see sin around every corner. Neither extreme is what we find modeled consistently in Scripture.

If anyone had a right to focus singularly on people's sin, it was Jesus. He was perfect himself, and knew—more completely than any of us—what was in the human heart (John 2:24–25). Nevertheless, throughout his ministry, Jesus not only revealed to people the depth of their sin, but he also recognized the depth of their suffering and met them with compassion:

> *And he went throughout all Galilee, teaching*
> *in their synagogues and proclaiming the gospel*
> *of the kingdom and healing every disease and*
> *every affliction among the people. So his fame*
> *spread throughout all Syria, and they brought*
> *him all the sick, those afflicted with various*
> *diseases and pains, those oppressed by demons,*
> *those having seizures, and paralytics, and he*
> *healed them.*
> *(Matt. 4:23–24)*

The opposite of this kind of compassion is displayed in Job's three friends: Eliphaz, Bildad, and Zophar. In studying through the book of Job a few years ago, I was deeply convicted (brokenhearted, really) as I came to realize how similar to these three friends' counsel my own counsel could tends to sound. Eli, Bill, and Zip don't seem to be unbiblical in their counsel. They continually pointed Job to God (e.g., 5:8–9; 8:20; 11:4–5), they repeatedly spurred Job on toward righteousness (e.g., 8:5–6; 11:14–15; 18:21), and they dug tirelessly to uncover the sin in Job's heart (e.g., 5:17; 11:6; 15:4–6; 22:1–11). Those are three points that would fit neatly into any biblical counseling or discipleship training I've ever attended!

So what were they missing? What was I missing? Ultimately, Eli, Bill, Zip, and I were all missing a robust appreciation of the complexity of suffering in our fallen world. We had developed an oversimplified understanding of how suffering and sin relate to each other. We had not appreciated all the different ways in which people can suffer that are *not* a result of their own personal sin. And we had failed to comprehend the complex hurt and pain people experience when some of God's greatest earthly blessings are taken from them. As a result, we had misunderstood the true nature of *both* suffering *and* sin.

We'll take a more in-depth look at sin in the next chapter, but we first need to try to gain a better understanding of the nature of suffering. Suffering is a significant component of the messes people find themselves in. And, as we will discuss in chapter 13, God addresses our suffering powerfully through the gospel. In Christ, God is not only redeeming our hearts and making them new, he is also redeeming our suffering. He is using that which is dark and evil on the face of it for our ultimate good and his ultimate glory. As we see countless times throughout the Psalms (e.g., 13; 22; 42; 62; 120), redemption begins with us being honest about our suffering—about the fact that it's real and that it really hurts.

SUFFERING AND OUR MESS

How *does* suffering contribute to the messes people find themselves in? If we are called to lovingly "gospel" others, the gospel is only a good solution if we have accurately identified the problem. So how do we understand the problem? If your friend is afraid of men, or anxious about work, or consumed with lustful thoughts, or depressed about a grade, or constantly yelling at his children, is that a suffering problem or a sin problem? The short answer is: both. As we will see, suffering and sin contribute to our messes in different ways, but they are almost always both contributing. Every person you minister to will inevitably be *both* a sufferer and a sinner.

Sometimes the suffering that people experience will be the direct result of their own sin. Sometimes Job's friends would be right. Of course, a broken clock is also right twice a day. There will inevitably be scenarios where a husband who cheated on his wife, left his family, and neglected his kids will be suffering loneliness, guilt, and maybe even an STD. The suffering he is experiencing is obviously a direct result of his own sinful thoughts, emotions, and actions.

However, oftentimes the connection won't be so obvious. And here's a good rule of thumb: unless the causative connection between a person's suffering and their sin is absolutely clear, don't even try to make a connection. Unless you *know* that the suffering someone is experiencing is a direct result of sin in their life, don't even speculate about possible connections between the two. Wisdom doesn't lead us to the kind of conjecture Job's friends engaged in. It leads us the other way. The truth is, suffering is so multifaceted and complex, there is almost certainly no simple connection to be found. So don't try.

Nevertheless, there are a few aspects of how suffering relates to a person's mess that *are* always true and *can* be helpful as we seek to love those around us. First, suffering always produces pressure that brings the contents of our hearts out into the open. As I mentioned back in chapter 6, one way to understand the relationship between our suffering and our sin is to think of it like a water bottle. If you smash a water bottle and water comes spraying out, it's because there was water in the bottle. The smashing simply brings out whatever is inside. If the bottle is full of air, air will come flying out; if the bottle is full of water, water will come flying out; if the bottle is full of spoiled milk . . . you get the picture.

Our responses to suffering tend to tell us more about the condition of our hearts than they do the condition of our circumstances. Does a burnt meal reduce you to tears? Our tears tend to reveal desires, hopes, and dreams. Has pressure at work led to excessive video gaming at home? Our choices tend to reveal the things we look to for hope and satisfaction. Has a friend's promotion captivated your mind with jealous daydreams? Our meditations tend to reveal our deepest longings.

But suffering is also much more than the pressure that forces our internal messes into the open. Suffering can also dramatically determine the shape of the mess as it comes out. We all have a multitude of shaping influences in our lives— the types of things that determine our tastes, our preferences, and the particular manifestations of our sin. But suffering is one of the strongest shaping influences we experience as humans. Suffering not only brings our internal mess out into the open, it also shapes what that mess looks like when it comes out.

It makes me think of the cookie press Christmas cookies I used to make with my mom when I was a kid. If you're not familiar with it, a cookie press is essentially like a large syringe, but instead of having a needle on the end you have a small disk with holes cut out in the shape of a design. As you push the dough through the disk, it comes out in whatever shape the holes are in, allowing you to make little cookies in the shape of a wreath, a snowflake, a star, etc. The shape of the disk determines the shape of the cookie.

Our suffering can be a lot like that. Depending on how, when, and to what degree you suffer, it changes the shape of the mess that comes out. It may not make it bigger or smaller, but it does impact what it looks like.

I used to love making those cookies with my mom. She was an incredible woman. She was my best friend and the anchor of my life. And ten years ago, when she passed away from cancer, losing her didn't only push the mess in my heart out into the open, it also deeply influenced the specific shape that mess takes whenever it comes out.

The experience of losing my mom is probably something that will impact the shape my outward sin takes for the rest of my life. Whenever my internal mess gets pushed out into the open, even now, it is tinged with the effects of that loss. It often looks fiercely independent because I can feel like I'm on my own; it often looks stoic because busyness was the way I coped. There are ways in which I will never "get over" that suffering. It will shape me for the rest of my life. Suffering shapes, in subtle and distinct ways, the various messes of all our lives.

And, beyond all of this, suffering is a mess in and of itself. This isn't simply because it brings our internal mess out into the open, or because it shapes and influences the way our mess is made manifest. Suffering is its own mess. This isn't the way it was supposed to be. As D. A. Carson so plainly puts it, "At the most basic level, suffering is to moral evil what cause is to effect; yet suffering itself is so tied to the fallen order that it too is rightly thought of as evil, and experienced as such."[2]

Suffering is evil. It is painful and difficult. It is the antithesis of how God created us to live in Eden and how he has promised that we will live eternally in heaven. It exists because of the reality of moral evil in our fallen world, through sin. And while each and every instance of suffering cannot—and should not—be traced back to a specific moral evil, the presence of moral evil in the world is why suffering exists.

Therefore, as we minister to those around us who are suffering, we are called to do more than point out the evil of sin in each unique situation; we are called to recognize and point out the evil of suffering as well. A hurricane that destroyed your house is heartbreaking, real, and evil in and of itself. The cultural system that denies you opportunities because of the color of your skin is heartbreaking, real, and evil in and of itself. The birth defect that keeps you confined to a wheelchair is heartbreaking, real, and evil in and of itself. The demands of your job that cause you to overwork for no additional pay are heartbreaking, real, and evil in and of themselves.

Now, calling suffering heartbreaking, real, and evil doesn't mean that it's not redeemable. It absolutely is! In Christ we have hope in the midst of our suffering that blows its negative impacts out of the water. But, while we'll talk about those biblical promises in a couple of chapters, applying gospel hope to the suffering in people's lives begins with recognizing the suffering in the first place. We all suffer in countless ways. And I'm afraid that one of the most significant reasons we fail to recognize suffering in the lives of those we're ministering to is because we're simply not used to looking for it.

THE WAYS WE SUFFER

When we think of suffering, we tend to think of large, tragic circumstances that are out of the norm. This leads us to assume that there are seasons of life when we are suffering and seasons when we are not. In the same way, we tend to categorize those we are ministering to as either "suffering" or "not suffering." If it's obvious that someone is suffering, we may respond with compassion and patient consideration, but if we don't think a person is really suffering, we tend to skip over this category completely and dive right into his or her sin. But this is based on an inaccurate understanding of the fallen world we live in, and the multitude of ways we are impacted by its evil. Every person is suffering every day. Sometimes we suffer in horrific, tragic ways, and sometimes we suffer in subtle, continuous ways. However, to think biblically about those we're ministering to, we have to understand the breadth of all the different ways they (and we) suffer.

WE SUFFER FROM FALLEN BODIES

We suffer in subtle ways from imbalanced hormones, low blood sugar, catching a virus, or not getting a good night's sleep. We suffer in tragic ways from lifelong disability, chronic pain, disease, cancer, and death. Because of our fallen bodies, each one of us will eventually die and every person we love will die as well. This is life in our fallen world. (Biblical examples: Gen. 5; Mark 2:4; 1 Tim. 5:23.)

WE SUFFER FROM A FALLEN ENVIRONMENT

We suffer in subtle ways from the pollution in our cities, the effects of climate change (whatever the cause), or the fact that our earth has limited resources. We suffer in tragic ways from hurricanes, tornadoes, wildfires, earthquakes, and floods. Because of the fall, our environmental system doesn't work the way it was designed to work, and we suffer the consequences. This is life in our fallen world. (Biblical examples: Gen. 3:17–18; Ruth 1:1; Acts 27:18–20.)

WE SUFFER FROM A FALLEN CULTURE

We suffer in subtle ways from the promotion of individualism, consumerism, eroticism, or the indwelling impact of systemic racism. We suffer in tragic ways from the acceptable persecution of Christians or the normalized violence against minorities by those in authority. We suffer from a divisive, tribal culture that tears apart the unity that Jesus himself prayed for (demonstrated by your emotional reaction to some of the items I just mentioned). This is life in our fallen world. (Biblical examples: Deut. 20:16–18; 1 Kings 11:1–8; Gal. 2:11–14.)

WE SUFFER FROM SATAN AND DEMONS

We suffer in subtle ways from the fact that Satan is the ruler of this present world and from the lies we are tempted to believe that he affirms and encourages. We suffer in tragic ways from the demon possession of some of those around us who don't know Christ, or from Satan's strong cultural influence. We suffer because he has convinced most of us that he's not really a problem. This is life in our fallen world. (Biblical examples: 1 Cor. 7:5; 2 Cor. 2:10–11; 1 Tim. 1:19–20.)

WE SUFFER FROM OTHERS' LIMITATIONS/IMPERFECTIONS

We suffer in subtle ways from the coworker who doesn't learn new things as quickly as we do or the person on the other end of the helpline who has an accent that is difficult to understand. We suffer in tragic ways from the CEO who was not aware enough to recognize sexual harassment in the workplace or the government officials who are not skilled enough to avoid a war. Because of the fall, people have all sorts of problems and limitations that, even if they're not sin, can still cause us to suffer significantly. This is life in our fallen world. (Biblical examples: John 12:16; Rom. 15:1; Col. 3:12–13.)

WE SUFFER FROM OTHERS' SIN

We suffer in subtle ways when others dismiss us, make fun of us, or neglect their God-given responsibilities to us. We suffer in tragic ways when people attack us, abuse us, or oppress us. Because of the fall, we live surrounded by other fallen people. Every single one of them sins every single day. Whether in small or grotesque ways, we regularly suffer from it. This is life in our fallen world. (Biblical examples: Matt. 18:15; Acts 7:54–60; 2 Cor. 11:12–14.)

There are not seasons in life when we are suffering and seasons in life when we are not. In a fallen world, we are *all always* suffering. We simply suffer to different degrees in different seasons. This is fundamentally important to recognize as you seek to love those around you in the midst of their mess. There is *never* a time when you should skip over the suffering that is contributing to a person's mess and focus only on their sin. To treat someone as a sinner but neglect the reality of their suffering would be just as unbiblical as treating someone as a sufferer but neglecting the reality of their sin.

Of course, these are all just general categories to help you recognize the extent of suffering that people are experiencing. But the suffering experienced by the person you are ministering to isn't general at all. It is very specific. It is made up of the specific pressures, the specific people, and the specific circumstances that define that person's daily reality. I don't know what they are, but you do. This is one of the reasons God has placed you in that person's life: to give them the courage to see the reality of the fallen world they live in.

Recognizing the Impact of Our Fallen World

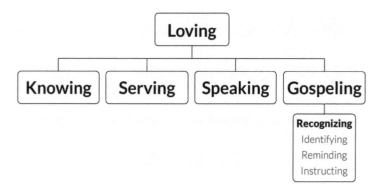

Recognizing the reality of our fallen world is a necessary part of gospeling another person. We can only understand the magnitude and impact of the good news if we have first understood the magnitude of the problem it addresses. And while the gospel *does* address the problem of our sin, it *also* addresses the problem of our suffering. As I've mentioned multiple times already, we are going to look at the hope of the gospel in a couple of chapters, but I don't want to rush into it too quickly. I'm afraid that rushing to the hope of the gospel is how many of us tend to address the suffering of those we're ministering to. We rush in with a verse, a promise, or a reminder, and in so doing we rush right past the suffering itself, not giving it the acknowledgment that something so devastating and significant deserves.

Maybe we do it because we want to make sure our ministry is "biblical." Maybe we do it because we don't like the uncomfortable reality of suffering ourselves. Maybe we do it because it's how others have ministered to us. Maybe we do it because we simply don't know what else to do. I mean, what else would you do? If you don't immediately run to gospel truth, aren't you simply encouraging the person to wallow in their pain?

While wallowing isn't the answer, there *is* an often-neglected biblical discipline that treats suffering honestly and prepares a person's heart to receive hope and truth. It's a biblical discipline we ought to slow down and invite sufferers into. It's the biblical discipline of lament.

Lament is an unfamiliar discipline for many Christians. One of the main reasons I think we neglect lament is because we view it as a synonym for complaining. And somewhere along the line we learned that complaining isn't a good thing. Maybe the Israelites in the wilderness come to mind. They grumbled and complained about all the things they had lost since leaving Egypt, they complained about the manna God provided, they complained about the quail God provided, and they were judged for it. Maybe Philippians 2:14 comes to mind, where Paul writes that we should "Do all things without grumbling or disputing."

But lamenting is fundamentally different from complaining. Complaining is making a grievance *about* God. Lamenting is making a grievance *to* God. In this way, lamenting is, ultimately, an act of faith. The most basic response to suffering we ought to invite others into is to cry out to God. In Psalm 13, David provides an example of lament. Note that this is a prayer that has been given to us in Scripture as an example to follow!

> *How long, O LORD? Will you forget me forever?*
> *How long will you hide your face from me?*
> *How long must I take counsel in my soul*
> *and have sorrow in my heart all the day?*
> *How long shall my enemy be exalted over me?*
>
> *(Ps. 13:1–2)*

This kind of honest cry in response to suffering is what prepares the psalmist's heart for the hope that comes next (vv. 5–6). The promises of the gospel don't penetrate to the depths of our sorrow unless we have first been honest about the reality of that sorrow. So, as you seek to love those around you who are suffering, take time to invite them to lament. Invite them to express to God the hurt, pain, and frustration they feel from all the external causes of their mess. And cry out with them. You should lament too. Seeing the suffering in their life will inevitably leave you sorrowful and pained as well. Cry out to God with them. Because, as you both lament, you will be turning to God in faith, prepared to receive the promises of redemption, renewal, and healing that can only be found in Christ. Echo, to them, the invitation that begins David Crowder's song "Come As You Are":

> *Come out of sadness, from wherever you've been*
> *Come brokenhearted, let rescue begin . . .*

ENDNOTES

1. Elyse Fitzpatrick and Dennis Johnson, *Counsel from the Cross*, 115.
2. D. A. Carson, *How Long, O Lord?*, 45.

CHAPTER 12

THE *Mess* INSIDE OF US

Gospeling, Part 2

Miles and I had been trying to connect for a couple of months. For one reason or another, we each had canceled on the other more than once, but we were finally able to get together one Monday afternoon. We met up at the church office and Miles began to describe the obsessive thoughts that had seemingly taken over his life.

Miles has three young children, and it was actually the behavior of one of his children where the whole story began. Miles's second son, Jonah, was about seven years old when he began developing certain tics. It started with eye-blinking but developed into head-twisting and throat-clearing at different points. Concerned about the health of his son, Miles did what any concerned parent of the twenty-first century would do: he googled it.

This led Miles down quite a rabbit hole. He read about tics in children, he read about tics in adults, he read about Tourette's syndrome, and he read about ADHD, OCD, and anxiety. As he read, Miles not only saw his son's struggles in the descriptions he was reading, he also saw many of his own. Ever since he was a child, Miles had struggled at different times with either tics or obsessive thoughts. This kind of struggle had taken over his life for a while in high school when he had become obsessed with his body image. Over the years, he had developed what he described as a number of different "mini health-phobias," and he had learned early on in his career that he needed to intentionally "unplug" from work, or his mind would simply never stop.

For most of the thirty-five years of his life, Miles had simply chalked these things up to his "perfectionist" personality. He just considered himself an intense and driven person. But now he was wondering if something was wrong—really wrong—not just with Jonah, but with him, too.

This is when the struggle really began. Miles began obsessing over his own mental health. Was he really sick? Did he have some kind of mental disease? Was there anything he could do about it? Was there any hope for a cure? Had he passed it on to his son? The questions got louder and louder as the days went by. As they did, the questions morphed into accusations. "You've *always* had this!" "You'll never get well!" "This will never go away!" And over time the accusations were accompanied by seemingly unrelated struggles, too. He would think, "If I can't control my innocent thoughts, then what can keep vulgar thoughts at bay?" And for the rest of the week he would be inundated with unwanted sexualized thoughts that were sickening to him, but that he couldn't seem to keep out of his mind.

As we sat there, Miles told me, "I just want to hear that this is not permanent, that I'm not stuck with this, and that there are biblical tools to make this go away." The pressure was on! While I listened to what Miles wanted from me, I began to pray, and to consider what he truly needed most. The truth was, I didn't have any quick fixes to make his obsessive thoughts go away. I didn't have any promises that he would never struggle with obsessive thoughts in the future. But what I did have was the ability to take him deeper, to help him understand what was contributing to his struggle, and to show him how God wanted to make him more like Christ through it. It was fair to assume that as he grew in Christlikeness, he would increase in his ability to take his thoughts captive. But the reduction of his obsessive thoughts would simply be a byproduct. God was after something far more fundamental.

Over our next few weeks, together we explored the different forms of suffering that were contributing to Miles's obsessive thoughts. His fallen body was a part of that. So was the fact that his mother had died of cancer when he was young, leading him to be extremely sensitive to his own health and that of his children. He had just come off a particularly intense year at work where high performance had been demanded of him almost constantly. And the seemingly endless amount of general and alarmist information online sure didn't help.

In addition to the external factors that contributed to Miles' struggle, we explored the internal contributors as well. Miles' fallen heart contributed in significant ways to the obsessions that were plaguing him. The truth was, Miles worshiped his health. He had come to believe that as long as he managed his physical health, he would be able to have the life he wanted both for himself and his family.

He also had a consuming desire for control. Miles did believe, theologically, that God is in control of everything. However, the truth was that, in his heart, Miles longed to be the one in control. Many of his obsessions were fueled by this desire to control the situation. The more he felt out of control, the worse the obsessions became. In fact, the whole reason Miles had come to talk to me in the first place was essentially so that he could regain control: "I just want to hear that this is not permanent, that I'm not stuck with this, and that there are biblical tools to make this go away."

These internal factors were at the root of the mess that was constantly bubbling up in Miles' mind. He was consumed by a desire for something God had not chosen to give him (control), and he was worshiping one of the blessings that God had given (his health). The Bible has a word to describe this kind of misplaced worship and life-ruling desire: sin.

Our Misunderstanding of Sin

What do you hear when I say, "Miles' sin was at the root of his struggle with obsessive thoughts"? I'm afraid that you may hear something like: "Miles has committed a specific sin, and that sin is the cause of his obsessions." While the first sentence is absolutely true, the second is overly simplistic, unbiblical, and harmful. But to identify the difference between the two, we don't need to dive into a debate over the nature of obsessive thoughts. We simply need a clearer definition of sin.

Too often, we define sin merely as the breaking of one of God's rules. Sin is what you call it when you lie to your mom. Sin is stealing from the office or cheating on a test. Sin is drinking too much or kissing the wrong person. We tend to think of sin as almost exclusively external. But sin goes much deeper. While lying, stealing, cheating, drunkenness, and adultery do all qualify as sins, in reality they're all just symptoms of something deeper. They are all the result of the indwelling sin in our hearts. This was one of the main points of Jesus' teaching as he repeatedly rebuked the Pharisees for their two-dimensional understanding that sin existed only on the surface:

> *Woe to you, scribes and Pharisees, hypocrites!*
> *For you clean the outside of the cup and the*
> *plate, but inside they are full of greed and self-*
> *indulgence. You blind Pharisee! First clean the*
> *inside of the cup and the plate, that the outside*
> *also may be clean.*
> *Woe to you, scribes and Pharisees, hypocrites!*
> *For you are like whitewashed tombs, which*
> *outwardly appear beautiful, but within are full of*
> *dead people's bones and all uncleanness. So you*
> *also outwardly appear righteous to others, but*
> *within you are full of hypocrisy and lawlessness.*
> *(Matt. 23:25–28)*

When we first moved into our house, our little 5,000 square foot lot had seven fully grown trees growing on it. We didn't have a backyard, we had a forest—an urban forest right smack dab in the middle of Los Angeles. The house got almost no direct sun, and the roots from the trees were coming up under the floorboards. Under the house, it was hard to tell the difference between an exposed root and a partially buried sewer line; I knew that the trees needed to go. So we had almost all of them taken out.

I soon began trying to figure out what we were going to do with our newly cleared plot of dirt. But before I could even put a plan in place, tiny little shoots began sprouting up all over the yard. I'd pull out five, and ten would come back in their place. I'd pull out ten, and twenty more would be there a week later. I finally tried digging down to figure out where they were coming from, only to find a root from one of the old trees with no fewer than fifty sprouts coming from where it had been cut off. And my backyard was *filled* with similarly cut-off roots.

That's what sin is like. Sin is not just the shoot. It's the entire system that is producing shoot after shoot. Removing each individual sprout that pops up doesn't actually do anything. It's like only cleaning the outside of a cup, or whitewashing a tomb. The problem is much deeper. The problem is inside. And in order to truly address the problem, you have to get to the root.

SIN AND OUR MESS

The Bible says the root of our sin resides in our hearts. Now, I'm not referring to the organ in your chest that pumps blood, of course. *The heart* is the biblical term used to describe your inner self. It houses your motivations, desires, will, and conscience. Essentially, your heart is the real you.

> As in water face reflects face,
> so the heart of man reflects the man.
>
> (Prov. 27:19)

This is why we are told to pay such close attention to the heart: because all of life, everything we do, flows out of it:

> Guard your heart above all else,
> for it determines the course of your life.
>
> (Prov. 4:23, NLT)

When you are overcome with anxiety, paralyzed by fear, consumed with anger, or your patience simply runs out, it's an overflow of your heart. When you get in a fight with someone, cheat on your taxes, look at pornography, or simply make an unkind joke, it's an overflow of your heart.

Without Christ, our hearts are turned in on themselves by sin. Self-satisfaction is our strongest desire. Self-esteem is our greatest need. Self-preservation is our ultimate goal. Self-promotion is our most familiar tool. In theological terms, we worship ourselves.

Our hearts were created to worship. God created us and established a relationship with us. But this is not a peer relationship; it is the relationship between a Creator and his creation. And at the very core of his creation is the compulsion to worship him as the Creator. However, ever since the fall, humans no longer naturally worship the Creator God; instead, our hearts have turned inward, compelled to seek our own power and glory (like Adam and Eve before us). The apostle Paul describes what this is like at the beginning of his letter to the Romans:

> For although they knew God, they did not honor
> him as God or give thanks to him, but they
> became futile in their thinking, and their foolish
> hearts were darkened. . . . Therefore God gave
> them up in the lusts of their hearts to impurity,
> to the dishonoring of their bodies among
> themselves, because they exchanged the truth
> about God for a lie and worshiped and served the
> creature rather than the Creator, who is blessed
> forever! Amen.
> (Rom. 1:21, 24–25)

When we worship the creature (ourselves) rather than the Creator, it naturally produces a certain kind of fruit in our lives. It produces anxiety, lust, selfishness, pride, self-pity, jealousy, anger, bitterness, impatience, and hate. This is the fruit of a heart darkened by self-worship. This is the true nature of sin.

However, in Christ, we have been given a new heart (Ezek. 36:26). We have been born again and are no longer enslaved to the fruit that previously characterized our lives. The thing we need to recognize, though, is that this new heart doesn't completely and absolutely replace the old one—at least, not yet. One way to think about it is that, on earth, Christians have a bipartite heart—a heart with two distinct parts. Part of your heart worships God and part of your heart worships yourself. This is why Paul's confession resonates so powerfully with us: "For I do not understand my own actions. For I do not do what I want, but I do the very thing I hate" (Rom. 7:15).

Every Christian constantly walks through life with mixed motives. And your life bears out this tension. This is why you can get so angry at other drivers on your way to volunteer at the homeless shelter. This is why your prayers for your roommate may devolve into self-pitying complaining. This is why you may find yourself yelling at your kids in the middle of family worship. If you are a follower of Christ there will inevitably be significant good fruit in your life, and there will also be a significant amount of ungodly fruit that continues to pour out of your not-yet-perfected heart.

We're like a tree with two sets of roots. One set of roots is healthy, producing good fruit (behaviors (B), thoughts (T), and emotions (E)) on some of the tree's branches. The other set of roots is unhealthy or dead, producing dead, rotten fruit (behaviors (B), thoughts (T), and emotions (E)) on other branches.

Growing in Christlikeness (as we will see in the next two chapters) is the process of the God-worshiping portion of your heart continually growing and displacing the self-worshiping portion of your heart. But, before we get there, we need to recognize that the darkened part of our heart that remains is no small problem. It's a huge issue.

We can tend to downplay the seriousness of sin. We may call sin unhealthy, unfortunate, or unhelpful. Or we call the fruit of sin simply a misunderstanding or a mistake. But sin is an offense against a holy God. It is wicked. It is evil.

How do you feel about calling the self-worshiping portion of a person's heart evil? Maybe you feel as uncomfortable as when

I called suffering evil in the previous chapter. In our culture, we tend to reserve the word "evil" for the killing of the innocent, the violating of the weak, or the particularly grotesque. And while those are all horrifically evil, we can't forget that God calls the indwelling sin in all of our hearts evil, too.

Paul calls our self-serving actions evil (Rom. 7:19–21) and he calls our self-serving desires evil (Col. 3:5). The writer of Hebrews warns us to pay close attention to ourselves, "lest there be in any of you an evil, unbelieving heart" (Heb. 3:12). And Jesus reminds us that whenever there is evil in a person's heart, what comes out in that person's life will be evil, too: "The good person out of the good treasure of his heart produces good, and the evil person out of his evil treasure produces evil" (Luke 6:45).

For Christians, good really does come out of the good and God-worshiping portion of our hearts. But becoming a Christian doesn't mean that our hearts, in this life, always and completely worship God. There is still a remnant of our self-worshiping hearts that has to be dealt with (Rom. 7:15–20; Col. 3:5; James 4:1). This self-worshiping part of our hearts isn't just sick or broken, it's evil, and the fruit it produces is evil as well. Our self-worship is evil because it is a blatant offense against the one true God who alone deserves all of our worship. It is an internal attempted coup d'état. We are not just trying to go around him. We are trying to dethrone him from the depths of our very souls.

Self-worship is essentially a breaking of the very first commandment: "You shall have no other gods before me" (Ex. 20:3). It is a breaking of what Jesus called the "greatest commandment": "And he said to him, 'You shall love the Lord your God with all your heart and with all your soul and with all your mind. This is the great and first commandment'" (Matt. 22:37–38).

Self-worship isn't just a small problem. It's not just an inconvenient issue. It's an overwhelming, gigantic mess. It wreaks havoc on a person's relationship with God, and it creates a completely overwhelming mess in their life as a result. Self-worship is at the root of what keeps a person from spending regular time with God in Scripture and in prayer. It's at the root of struggles with eating, struggles with drugs, and struggles with relationships. It's at the root of loud explosive rage and quiet seething anger. It's at the root of hopeless disappointment and paralyzing fear. The evil of self-worship is quite a mess.

Thankfully, in Christ, our self-worship is not the end of the story. The One we have sought to dethrone by force voluntarily came down from his throne so that we might be forgiven, redeemed, reborn, and adopted into his family. We're going to take a deeper look at the beauty of this good news in the next chapter. But first, if we're going to help others understand the magnitude of the gospel, we need to start by helping them understand the magnitude of the problem Christ came to address. Understanding self-worship can help us do that, but not if it stays theoretical. In order for the gospel to penetrate deep into a person's heart, we need to help them identify the practical ways in which self-worship is manifesting itself in their life.

The Ways We Sin

If sin is ultimately rooted in self-worship, how should we understand the connection between those deep motivations and the thoughts we think, emotions we feel, and actions we take every day? How do we help others understand the depth of their sin not just in a theoretical way, but in a truly practical and penetrating way?

Scripture uses numerous concepts and analogies to help us understand the ways self-worship comes out in our lives. Idolatry is the most common concept we find in the Old Testament. And in the New Testament, the most common concept we find is that of life-ruling "desires."[1] The two concepts of "idolatry" and "desires" work together to help us understand how the sin in our hearts connects to the external sins we commit.

We all have desires. We can have desires for good and godly things, and we can have desires for bad and sinful things. Pretty simple, right? Many of us assume that as long as you follow your desires for good things and deny your desires for bad things, you're in the clear.

But God isn't only concerned with the *objects* of our desire, he is also concerned with the *degree* of our desire. The only reason you would indulge in a sinful desire (like adultery) is because your desire for that object or experience (sex) is greater than your desire for God. Scripture often calls this replacement of God "idolatry." But God is offended not only when your desire for *sin* is greater than your desire for him; he is offended when your desire for *anything* is greater than your desire for him.

Idolatry is not only the desiring of bad things; it is also when a desire for good things turns bad. If you are married, your desire for your spouse is a good and godly desire. But if your desire for your spouse becomes greater than your desire for God, that, *too,* is idolatry. Stuart Scott's definition of an idol is one I have used for years: "An idol is anything that we consistently make equal to or more important than God in our attention, desire, devotion, or choices."[2] Gregory Beale also provides a helpful definition, developed from Martin Luther's comments on the first commandment: "Whatever your heart clings to or relies on for ultimate security, that is your God."[3]

According to these definitions, you can essentially make an idol out of anything. Your job or your education, your family or your friends, your home or your car, the city you live in or the town you grew up in, your vacations or your favorite food, your comfort or your reputation, power or control, romance or success: they could all be idols. And every one of your idols has one fundamental thing in common: you. They all serve you. The only reason you're clinging to them, the only reason you're relying on them for ultimate security, the only reason you are consistently making them equal to or more important than God, is because, deep down, you believe they'll deliver what you desire.

Every specific idol in our lives is simply a display of our self-worship pushed through the filter of our personal desires.

This means that, as we come to worship God more and more (and therefore ourselves less and less), we will naturally abandon our idols along the way. However, this also means that spiritual transformation is about more than simply abandoning one's idols. It's about addressing the self-worship that is at the root of it all. You see, we can set aside specific idols for all sorts of different reasons. Sometimes people will abandon their idols out of genuine repentance (which we will talk about in chapter 14), but sometimes they will abandon their idols simply because their desires have changed.

Just because a person has changed, doesn't mean their heart has genuinely been transformed. Just because their actions are different, doesn't mean they have truly been captivated by the glory and grace of God. Maybe they finally stopped smoking. Maybe they gave up pornography. Maybe they began going to the gym. Maybe they started teaching Sunday school. But, if we want to provide genuine gospel care, we have to ask: Why?

When a person's desires change, they will naturally turn away from the idols they used to cling to. However, turning away from a particular sin because your desires change isn't spiritual transformation; it's just idol-swapping. Maybe a person has swapped out the idol of alcohol for the idol of career success because he has come to desire the benefits brought by money more than the benefits brought by drunkenness. Or maybe he's swapped out the idol of career success for the idol of physical health because he has a newfound desire to live longer. The specific idols may be different, but the god of "self" is still on the throne.

God is after more than just change for change's sake. He wants more than lives that just look more "Christian." He's after transformation. But for transformation to happen, it must start with recognizing that the problem is deeper than we tend to realize. The problem isn't just that we're doing the wrong things or thinking the wrong things. It isn't just that we have the wrong desires. God is calling his people to do more than simply swap out their desires. He wants to reorient our worship.

The reorientation of a person's worship begins with helping them trace their sinful behaviors, thoughts, and emotions back to the idols they've turned to, the desires that are motivating those idols, and ultimately the self-worship that is at the root of it all.

SINFUL BEHAVIORS

The sinful things we do are rooted in our self-worship. Why would a woman verbally abuse her coworker? Maybe one of her greatest desires is to impress her boss. When her self-worship gets pressed through this desire, it creates the mini-god of efficiency. The god of efficiency demands results from her coworkers where the God of the universe would command love.

Or why would a teenager begin experimenting sexually with different friends? Maybe she longs for comfort, acceptance, and belonging. When her self-worship gets pressed through these desires, it creates the mini-god of sexual pleasure. The god of sexual-pleasure demands indulgence where the God of the universe commands self-control.

SINFUL THOUGHTS

The sinful things we think are also rooted in our self-worship. Why would a man spend all his free time thinking about ways to maximize his finances and neglect thinking about his relationships with his family, church community, and neighbors? Maybe he has always desired security and the toys money can buy. When his self-worship gets pressed through this desire, it creates the mini-god of money. The god of money demands attention and devotion that the God of the universe commands for himself alone.

Or why would an elderly gentleman spend his days thinking about the past and distracting himself from the present? Maybe he has a desire for countless things that are all wrapped up in "the way it used to be." When his self-worship gets pressed though this desire, it creates the mini-god of nostalgia. The god of nostalgia demands his constant meditation which the God of the universe commands be directed to his Word.

SINFUL EMOTIONS

Even the sinful things we feel are rooted in our self-worship. This one might be a little more controversial, but let's think about it for a second. Can emotions really be sinful? The short answer is: absolutely. Scripture clearly equates many emotional words with sin: envy (Mark 7:22), jealousy (Rom. 13:13), anger (Gal. 5:20), coveting (Ex. 20:17), anxiety (Matt. 6:25), etc. While there are "holy" versions of some of these emotions (Ps. 139:19–22;

Phil. 2:28), more often than not we experience them not as an overflow of our love for God but as an overflow of our love for ourselves.

Why would a man be overcome with hopelessness and anxiety after the loss of his job? Maybe he has long desired a certain career path, financial security, and the social status his job provided. When his self-worship gets pressed though these desires, it creates the mini-god of career. The god of career demands a clear plan and the power to execute it, while the God of the universe declares himself alone to be sovereign.

Or why would a woman be consumed with anger at her mother? Maybe she desires respect, autonomy, and relational intimacy. When her self-worship gets pressed through these desires, it creates the mini-god of an imagined relationship that her mother can't (or won't) give her. The god of this imagined relationship demands everyone's complete allegiance before it will deliver its promises, while the God of the universe offers respect and intimacy simply by grace.

Helping each one of these people to see the ways in which self-worship is motivating their behaviors, thoughts, and emotions would help them see that the problem of sin is much deeper than we tend to think. To do this you don't need to identify every possible idol a person may be struggling with. The specific idols aren't the root of the problem. Nonetheless, identifying some of them along the way (and the desires that motivate them) can help a person recognize the self-worship that can be so difficult to see. Self-worship is the root cause of our internal mess. But most of the time it is unrecognizable to our own eyes. It's hard (if not impossible) to accurately evaluate our own hearts. "The heart is deceitful above all things . . . " (Jer. 17:9). This is why we need each other. As Paul Tripp observes,

> *I need you in order to really see and know myself.*
> *Otherwise, I will listen to my own arguments, believe*
> *my own lies, and buy into my own delusions. My self-*
> *perception is as accurate as a carnival mirror. If I am going*
> *to see myself clearly, I need you to hold the mirror of God's*
> *Word in front of me.*[4]

IDENTIFYING THE DEPTH OF OUR FALLEN HEARTS

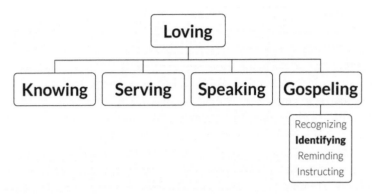

The people you are ministering to need you to hold the mirror of God's Word in front of them. This is what love does. It's not always easy, and it's almost never fun, but it's a profound act of love to help others see themselves more accurately so that they might appreciate the gospel more deeply. They need you to help them see the idols and desires that they can't see on their own. They need you to help them identify the depth of the fallenness of their hearts.

Again, we can only understand the magnitude and impact of the good news if we have first understood the magnitude of the problem it addresses. Good news is only as good as the problem it addresses is bad. Someone paying off your credit card debt is great if you think you owe $100. But someone paying off your credit card debt is unbelievable when you realize you actually owe $100,000! As Jesus put it, "He who is forgiven little, loves little" (Luke 7:47).

This is why I believe it's so important to help others identify the self-worship still residing in their hearts. Essentially what we are doing is inviting them into confession. In confession, we invite a person to recognize their self-worship before both God (1 John 1:9) and us (James 5:16). The purpose of confession is not condemnation or judgment, but, again, so that they might appreciate anew the glorious grace of Christ.

Confession is about more than simply admitting the wrong things we've done. It's about agreeing with God that a significant portion of our heart is still turned inward, worshiping ourselves. It's agreeing with God that our sin goes deeper than we had previously realized. We will spend the rest of our lives confessing in this way. This is not a one-time event, but a spiritual discipline to be developed. As Tim Keller explains,

There's a certain sense in which we spend our entire lives thinking we've reached the bottom of our hearts and finding it is a false bottom. Mature Christians are not people who have completely hit bedrock. I do not believe that is possible in this life. Rather, they are the people who know how to keep drilling and are getting closer and closer.[5]

In the same vein, just as we invite others to echo David's prayers of lament in the Psalms, we should also invite them to echo his prayer that longs for deeper confession.

Search me, O God, and know my heart!
Try me and know my thoughts!
And see if there be any grievous way in me,
and lead me in the way everlasting!

(Ps. 139:23–24)

If those you are ministering to will pray this prayer, I promise you that God will answer it. He will pull back the curtain on their hearts and expose their self-worship in the ways that only he can. He will lay them bare. But he won't leave them alone. He will cover them with his mercy and surround them with his grace. He will come alongside them with compassion and overwhelm them with blessing.

It's been a rough couple of chapters. I don't know how you're feeling, but, as I bring the writing of these two chapters to a close, my heart feels heavy. It's not easy looking honestly at the reality of our fallen world and the reality of our fallen hearts, but it's important that we do so. It's necessary if I'm going to love you well, as an author; and it's necessary if you're going to love those around you well, as a friend.

Every messy person in your life needs to be shown that the mess is, in fact, worse than they ever knew. And every messy person in your life needs to be shown that, consequently, the gospel is greater than they ever imagined. As we closed the last chapter, I shared with you the invitation that begins the song

"Come As You Are." It continues with not only an additional invitation, but a promise as well:

Come find your mercy, O sinner come kneel.
Earth has no sorrow that heaven can't heal.

In the face of the evil of suffering and the evil of sin, this is the promise we will explore in the next chapter, the promise of the gospel: that earth has no sorrow that heaven can't heal.

ENDNOTES

1. David Powlison, "Idols of the Heart and Vanity Fair," Journal of Biblical Counseling.
2. Stuart Scott, *The Exemplary Husband*, 91.
3. G. K. Beale, *We Become What We Worship*, 17.
4. Paul Tripp, *Instruments in the Redeemer's Hands*, 54.
5. Tim Keller, *Counterfeit Gods*, 176.

CHAPTER 13

TELL ME THE OLD, OLD STORY

Gospeling, Part 3

Lisa's struggles weren't all that different from those of many other young women in her situation. She had a demanding job, a complicated family, and a heart to serve others. Juggling these types of pressures seemed to be common among her friends, which left her wondering why she was having such a hard time handling it all. While Lisa had always been a generally anxious person with perfectionist tendencies, it seemed like things were only getting worse.

Lisa was anxious about everything—constantly feeling like she was failing. While she loved her job, the administrative load that came with it never seemed to end. While she loved her mom, the constant questions about when she was going to get married, or when she was going to move closer to home, gnawed at her. And while she treasured the opportunities she had to volunteer at church and with her old campus ministry, people always seemed to want more than she was able to give.

As a result, Lisa's anxiety and stress continued to grow. Some days the pressure was so overwhelming she could barely get to work, let alone deal with anything else. She had begun to have periodic panic attacks triggered by all sorts of things: an email from a church leader, a text from her mom, or even just the fact that it was Monday morning.

Lisa didn't know what to do. Thankfully, she felt comfortable enough to reach out and ask for help. When Lisa and I met up at a coffee shop, along with her community group leader, Estela, her goal was obvious. At this point in the book, you may be able to guess it yourself. Lisa wanted me and Estela to help her figure out how to manage life and make it all work. She wanted a plan to get everything done without this pesky "anxiety" issue getting in the way. She wanted to be fixed.

But, as we've seen in the past two chapters, Lisa's problem (like all of our problems) went deeper than she realized. It wasn't something that could just be fixed. There wasn't some simple life hack she was missing. Lisa's stress, anxiety, panic attacks, and all the rest were the predictable result of the mess (both internal and external) in her life. There was the external mess caused by the pressure of her job, her mother's unrealistic expectations, and the demands of overly programmed ministries. And there was the internal mess caused by her idolatry of control, her unwillingness to accept the magnitude of God's grace, and her unrealistic expectations of herself. The problem was bigger than she even knew.

What, then, did Lisa need? More than a better scheduling system, more than healthy boundaries with her parents, more than a new job or fewer volunteer commitments, Lisa needed the gospel.

Gospel Truth

It might sound strange to hear me say that Lisa needed the gospel. Too often, we assume that the only people in need of the gospel are non-Christians. You may even be thinking that it is insulting to claim that Lisa needed the gospel, as if I was questioning the genuineness of her faith. But, as I've said before, the gospel isn't only what non-Christians need in order to be reconciled to God. The gospel is also what every Christian needs every day to continue to grow in Christlikeness. What every Christian needs in every one of life's messes is gospel truth.

Of course, there is more that we need to hear than simply reminders of the gospel—such as reminders of how God wants us to live as his children (and that's what we're going to explore in the next chapter). But being reminded about the enormity of God's grace should always precede being reminded about the immensity of his call. This is why much of the New Testament is structured the way it is (gospel truth: Eph. 1–3; Rom. 1–11; Col. 1–2; before gospel commands: Eph. 4–6; Rom. 12–16; Col. 3–4). Before we can learn *how* to live, we must be clear on *why* we should want to live that way in the first place. Gospel truth always comes before gospel commands.

But what do I mean by gospel truth? As I mentioned back in chapter 2, gospel truth includes both the message and the implications of the gospel for all those who have trusted in Christ. It includes all the truth about who God is, what he has done, who we are in Christ, what he has promised, and who he has created (and re-created) us to be. While you could call all of this simply "truth," the reason I call it "gospel truth" is because without the gospel this truth is not comforting at all; in fact, it's terrifying.

The gospel is the only thing that makes who God is, who we are, and what he has promised for us, good news. Without our reconciliation to God through faith in Christ, the truth about God is frightening, the truth about ourselves is mortifying, and the truth about what he has promised for us is devastating. But the gospel changes everything.

Therefore, the gospel is what we, as Christians, need to be reminded of over and over again. Regular reminders of the gospel re-captivate our hearts with the glory, beauty, and love of God and inspire the only thing that can truly transform our hearts: genuine worship of God. One of the most helpful modern resources I have found for regularly reminding myself, and others, of gospel truth is a little book by Milton Vincent called *A Gospel Primer*.[1] I'm going to reference it a few times in this chapter and the next, but it begins with this simple observation: "The New Testament teaches that Christians ought to hear the gospel as much as non-Christians do . . . Re-teaching the gospel and then showing how it applied to life was Paul's choice method for ministering to believers, thereby providing a divinely inspired pattern for me to follow when ministering to myself and to other believers."[2]

My soul craves reminders of gospel truth every single day. And so does the soul of the person you are ministering to. Again, what every Christian needs in every one of life's messes is gospel truth. Matt Chandler compares these needed gospel reminders to a popular song that comes on the radio.[3] After hearing just the first few notes, you change the station because you've heard it before and it's not really your thing. Again and again it comes on, and again and again you tune it out—until the one time you actually listen to the whole song, only to realize that not only do you *love* the song, but it communicates something powerful and moving to the depths of your heart. Gospel truth is just like that song, so don't let those you're ministering to change the channel until they've listened, really listened, to the whole thing.

GOSPEL TRUTH FOR OUR SUFFERING

Over the past couple of chapters, we have looked at how the mess in our lives comes from both inside and outside us. While you may be more familiar with the idea of applying gospel truth to sin, how does gospel truth speak to the suffering we face in a fallen world? As I said, gospel truth includes all the truth about who God is, what he has done, who we are in Christ, what he has promised, and who he has created (and re-created) us to be. When we're hurting or grieving, this is the truth we most desperately need. In the midst of a fallen and horribly broken world, gospel truth gives us hope, comfort, and even joy in the midst of pain. There are countless life-giving gospel truths we could turn to, but, to help you understand what I mean, let's look at three quick examples.

GOD UNDERSTANDS

The gospel reminds us that, no matter what we're going through, God understands. In Jesus' earthly life, he experienced the fullness of humanity, including the fullness of suffering (greater emotional pain, relational pain, and physical pain than we could ever imagine). Whether we're in the midst of a battle with cancer, a fight with a family member, the pressures of college, or a bad work environment, Jesus knows what we're experiencing. There is no suffering in our lives he cannot completely empathize with. "Since then we have a great high priest who has passed through the heavens, Jesus, the Son of God, let us hold fast our confession. For we do not have a high priest who is unable to sympathize with our weaknesses, but one who in every respect has been tempted as we are, yet without sin" (Heb. 4:14–15).

The fact that Jesus can empathize with all of our suffering and every one of our weaknesses reminds us that we can approach God intimately, not as some distant deity but as a loving father: "Let us then with confidence draw near to the throne of grace, that we may receive mercy and find grace to help in time of need" (Heb. 4:16).

This leads us to a second truth that the gospel reminds us of.

GOD IS WITH US

The gospel reminds us that, no matter what we're going through, God is with us. One of the most devastating parts of the suffering we experience is the isolation that comes with it. Suffering not only tempts us to believe that no one understands, it also convinces us that no one cares. We feel alone.

But God meets us in the depths of our suffering not only with grace and love, but also with his intimate presence (John 14:16–17; Matt. 28:20). This is why Psalm 23 is such a powerful salve for so many in times of trouble. It reminds us of the truth that we are *not* alone. We are *not* abandoned. In fact, whatever the situation, we are being led, loved, and comforted by God himself.

> *The LORD is my shepherd; I shall not want.*
> *He makes me lie down in green pastures.*
> *He leads me beside still waters.*
> *He restores my soul.*
> *He leads me in paths of righteousness*
> *for his name's sake.*
> *Even though I walk through the valley of the shadow of death,*
> *I will fear no evil,*
> *for you are with me;*
> *your rod and your staff,*
> *they comfort me.*
>
> *(Ps. 23:1–4)*

"Even though_____, you are with me." You can fill in the blank with any circumstance in your life. It is always true.

GOD IS REDEEMING OUR SUFFERING

Third, the gospel reminds us that no matter what we're going through, God is redeeming it for our good. Suffering never feels good. In the midst of it, it's hard to imagine how it could ever possibly be used for good. Yet this is the hope God gives us in the gospel. Grumpy coworkers can be redeemed. The impact of a technology-obsessed culture can be redeemed. Financial troubles can be redeemed. Chronic illness can be redeemed. Even the most devastating moments of our lives can be redeemed.

Back in chapter 9, we looked at God's promise that he will redeem *everything* that happens to us, including our suffering: "And we know that for those who love God *all things* work together for good, for those who are called according to his purpose" (Rom. 8:28). While simply quoting this verse to someone who is suffering may not be the most loving application of truth, helping them wrestle with the truth behind it can be a transformative experience.

When someone really wrestles with God's promise to redeem our suffering, what they are ultimately looking for is the proof that it is true—which leads them right back to the gospel. In fact, the gospel was the proof that Paul himself used to demonstrate that God could be trusted to fulfill such an enormous promise. Just a few verses later, he continues, "What then shall we say to these things? If God is for us, who can be against us? He who did not spare his own Son but gave him up for us all, how will he not also with him graciously give us all things?" (Rom. 8:31–32). As D. A. Carson summarizes,

> *In the darkest night of the soul, Christians have something to hang onto that Job never knew. We know Christ crucified. Christians have learned that when there seems to be no other evidence of God's love, they cannot escape the Cross.*[4]

The gospel proves that God can be trusted. The gospel demonstrates the extent of God's love, the magnitude of his power, and the wisdom of his plan. This means that, no matter what kind of suffering we're going through, no matter how long, no matter how painful, no matter how disappointing, we can know that the triune God understands, that he will never leave us, and that he will ultimately redeem it all for our good.

This overwhelming hope and comfort is true for us because of our identity in Christ. It is ours through the gospel.

And in the gospel, God not only promises to redeem the effects of our fallen world; he promises to redeem our fallen hearts as well.

GOSPEL TRUTH FOR OUR SIN

In the last chapter, we talked about the fact that our sin goes far deeper than we realize. The problem isn't simply our lying, stealing, cheating, drunkenness, or adultery; it's the self-worship that is motivating it all. But God meets us in the depths of our self-worship with more grace than we could ever imagine. In Christ, he points to all of the ugly, deceitful, self-glorifying parts of our hearts and declares, "And such were some of you. But you were washed, you were sanctified, you were justified in the name of the Lord Jesus Christ and by the Spirit of our God" (1 Cor. 6:11).

You may still struggle with residual self-worship in your heart, but that is not who you truly are. That is not your new identity. In Christ you have been forgiven. In Christ you have been redeemed. In Christ you have been washed clean. The gospel announces all of these blessings, and so much more! Whatever the depth of your sin, it is never beyond the reach of God's grace in Christ.

There are numerous places throughout the New Testament that reveal the magnitude of God's grace in the midst of our sin. But none is more overwhelming, at least to my eyes, than the first chapters of Ephesians. Let's just look at how the book begins:

> Blessed be the God and Father of our
> Lord Jesus Christ, who has blessed us in
> Christ with every spiritual blessing in the
> heavenly places, even as he chose us in
> him before the foundation of the world,
> that we should be holy and blameless
> before him. In love he predestined us for
> adoption to himself as sons through Jesus
> Christ, according to the purpose of his will,
> to the praise of his glorious grace, with
> which he has blessed us in the Beloved.
> In him we have redemption through his
> blood, the forgiveness of our trespasses,
> according to the riches of his grace, which
> he lavished upon us, in all wisdom and

insight making known to us the mystery of
his will, according to his purpose, which he
set forth in Christ as a plan for the fullness
of time, to unite all things in him, things
in heaven and things on earth.
    In him we have obtained an inheritance,
having been predestined according to
the purpose of him who works all things
according to the counsel of his will, so
that we who were the first to hope in
Christ might be to the praise of his glory.
In him you also, when you heard the word
of truth, the gospel of your salvation,
and believed in him, were sealed with the
promised Holy Spirit, who is the guarantee
of our inheritance until we acquire
possession of it, to the praise of his glory.

(Eph. 1:3–14)

What comes to mind when you think about the gospel? I'm afraid that many of us tend to think of one or two aspects of God's grace that we learned early on in our Christian lives and just keep coming back to. I know that's what I tend to do. Maybe "forgiveness" is what comes to mind when you think of the blessings of the gospel. Maybe it's "a relationship with God."

While both forgiveness and a relationship with God are huge gospel blessings, they are only the tip of the iceberg! In Christ we're not given only a few spiritual blessings, we have been given "every spiritual blessing in the heavenly places." Just looking through these twelve verses gives us a list of at least eleven different incredible blessings we receive through the gospel. In Christ you are:

- Chosen
- Holy
- Blameless
- Adopted
- Redeemed
- Forgiven

- Given purpose
- United
- An heir
- Sealed/guaranteed
- Indwelt by the Holy Spirit

As you continue on through chapters 2 and 3 of Ephesians you will discover that you are also:

- Made alive (2:4–5)
- Saved (2:5)
- Seated with Christ in heaven (2:6)
- Resurrected (2:6)
- Gifted grace (2:8–9)
- Prepared for good works (2:10)
- Reconciled (2:13)
- United across historical/ethnic divisions (2:14–16)
- A partaker of the promise (3:6)
- A revealer of the wisdom of God (3:10)
- Given bold access to God (3:12)

This list could go on and on, and throughout the New Testament it does. However, the point isn't to make the longest list possible. Long lists don't transform people's hearts. It's meditation upon what is *on* the list that changes us from the inside out. The gospel changes our identity. It acknowledges who we were and overwhelms us with gracious declarations of who we now are in Christ. Nothing can more powerfully transform our hearts than a slow, prayerful study of who we are in Christ, and what that says about the nature of our God.

Learning these truths for the first time is amazing, but learning them once is never enough. We all need to be constantly reminded of this new identity because of the deceitful sin that still indwells our hearts. The self-worshiping portion of our hearts tempts us to believe that we are still the hopeless sinners we once were. It spits out lies about our failures and confirms our suspicions about our lingering condemnation. It tempts us to think of ourselves as spiritually poor when, in fact, we are unimaginably rich.

We can never live up to the standards set by our self-worshiping hearts. They produce no grace, only guilt. They lead us to live like a homeless billionaire—living on the streets and scavenging through dumpsters because he has forgotten about his wealth. Just because the billionaire's wealth is stored in the bank (and not physically in his pockets) doesn't mean it's not real.

In the same way, just because our spiritual blessings are kept secure in the heavenly places doesn't mean they're any less real or consequential for our lives. The declarations of Ephesians 1–3 aren't just some fairytale. They are the pronouncement of who we *truly* are in Christ. The depth of our sin may be deeper than we ever knew, but that just means that the magnitude of God's grace is greater than we've ever imagined.

RENEWED WORSHIP

With all this talk about gospel truth it could be easy to focus so much on the individual truths that we forget what they are ultimately about. You see, there's no magic in the truths themselves. You could recite truths all day, you could memorize them, or you could chant them (and many people have), but the truths themselves have no power to change any of us. The power lies in the God that the truths describe. God himself is what we are after.

Yes, God has chosen to reveal himself to us through Scripture, but the gospel truth found in the Word only matters because it is *his* Word. As Jesus warned the religious people of his own day, "You search the Scriptures because you think that in them you have eternal life; and it is they that bear witness about me" (John 5:39). Jesus himself is the way, the truth, and the life (John 14:6). He himself is the bread of life (John 6:35), the good shepherd (John 10:11), and the light of the world (John 8:12). It is not the Bible or gospel truth, in a vacuum, that grants us everything we need for life. It's him (2 Peter 1:3). As God's Word, Scripture is his revelation of himself. Through it, we come to know *him* more completely, love *him* more fully, and be ever more captivated by *his* glory.

As such, what transforms our hearts from the inside out is not the intellectual enlightenment that comes from interacting with truth. What transforms our hearts is the worship that comes from an interaction with the God of the universe. This is what makes gospel truth so unique. Other truth may be able to help us, guide us, or encourage us, but only gospel truth can transform us. Because only gospel truth inspires genuine God-worship in us.

If self-worship is our deepest problem, it can't be dealt with simply by the strength of our will. You can't decide one day to simply stop worshiping yourself. The only way self-worship will become a smaller and smaller portion of our hearts is if it is constantly being displaced by God-worship. The hotter our worship of God burns, the more of our self-worship it will consume.

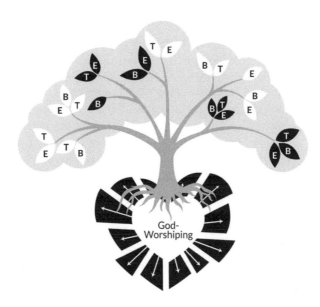

Theoretically, this shouldn't be that difficult. After all, given the choice between the glory of God and the glory of you, there's not really much of a competition. It's kind of like the Lakers playing a basketball game against my six-year-old daughter's playgroup (but even more lopsided!). All we need to do is take our eyes off ourselves long enough to catch a glimpse of the glory of God and the magnitude of his grace, and we will naturally be captivated to worship him. We just need to look up long enough to catch that glimpse.

Most of the time, though, we walk through life like a teenager immersed in crushing candies on his phone while he stands on the edge of the Grand Canyon. I'll never forget standing on an outcrop of rocks at the rim of the Grand Canyon. It's literally breathtaking. But in order to have your breath taken away, you have to look up from your phone. You have to do more than glance now and then while you stay absorbed in the game. You have to turn your attention to taking in the magnitude and beauty before you.

When I talk about being reminded of gospel truth, *that's* what I'm referring to. It's what the Bible calls *"renewing your mind" (Eph. 4:23; Rom. 12:2).*

As we walk through life, the natural inclination of our hearts is to turn inward, being captivated by ourselves. We all need our minds renewed daily, hourly, even minute by minute, so that we might take our eyes off ourselves long enough to be captivated by the glorious beauty and power of the God who stands before us.

This is why Paul tells the Ephesians that, as those who possess all the spiritual blessings we just looked at, they need to constantly be "renewed in the spirit of [their] minds." You may be familiar with Paul's instruction for Christians to "put off" the old self and "put on" the new self (which we'll look at in the next chapter), but, in order to make this kind of outward transformation possible, we can't neglect the regular mind renewal that's required:

> ... *to put off your old self, which belongs to your former manner of life and is corrupt through deceitful desires, and to be renewed in the spirit of your minds, and to put on the new self, created after the likeness of God in true righteousness and holiness.*
>
> *(Eph. 4:22–24)*

Earlier, in his letter to the Romans, Paul made this connection between the renewal of our minds and the transformation of our hearts explicit when he instructed them:

> *Do not be conformed to this world, but be transformed by the renewal of your mind.*
>
> *(Rom. 12:2)*

Renewing our minds with gospel truth inspires the worship of God that displaces our self-worship. Through the renewing of our minds, God captivates our hearts again and draws us into the worship that he alone deserves. God-worship can't be willed, and it can't be forced. It must be inspired by setting our minds on the glorious truths of the gospel. "The gospel reveals to me the breathtaking glory and loveliness of God, and in so doing, it lures my heart away from love of self and leaves me enthralled by Him instead."[5]

This is why, if we are to love others well, we *must* help them renew their minds. We must seek to inspire this kind of God-worship in their hearts. We must remind them of gospel truth.

REMINDING OF GOSPEL TRUTH

As you disciple and counsel those who are hurting and struggling, there is nothing they will need more than reminders of gospel truth. I know that over these last thirteen chapters I've said a lot of things are "very important" and "necessary" to loving one another well. But reminding others of gospel truth is unique. You could get everything else right, but if you don't remind the person you're ministering to of gospel truth, it's all just window-dressing. This is the reason Peter told his readers that he would remind them of gospel truth for as long as he was alive: "Therefore I intend *always to remind you* of these qualities, though you know them and are established in the truth that you have. I think it right, as long as I am in this body, to *stir you up by way of reminder*" (2 Peter 1:12–13).

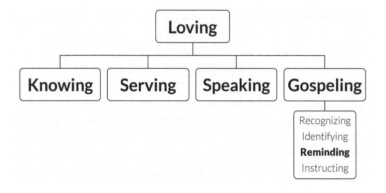

This is our call, as those who are engaged in gospel care, to constantly remind others of gospel truth. There is no other way to combat the lies and doubts that plague their minds. There is no other way to inspire genuine worship of God in their hearts. There is no other way to help them grow in Christlikeness. We must regularly—even daily—help remind them of gospel truth.

There are all sorts of different ways to go about this. Probably one of the simplest and most effective ways to remind someone of gospel truth is simply to sit down and walk through Scripture together. Gospel truth can come from any portion of Scripture. All you have to do is take the time to study it, interpret it, and meditate on the significance of it in light of the gospel.

When Estela and I met with Lisa, this was one of the main things we spent our time doing. In fact, it was Ephesians 1 that we studied together. We went through it slowly, looking deeply into each spiritual blessing that Paul lists, and discussing how the reality of those blessings combated the lies that were dominating Lisa's thoughts. As we did so, Lisa's eyes began to slowly lift off of herself as she was captivated more and more by the beauty and glory of God. Yet, admittedly, it was slow going.

But do you know what caused a breakthrough for Lisa? It wasn't the beginning of Ephesians. It was the story of Hannah at the beginning of 1 Samuel. During the time in between our meetings, Lisa and Estela had gotten together, and Estela had shared something she had read in her daily Bible reading. The passage Estela had read was from 1 Samuel 1, and it told the story of God's faithfulness to Hannah—and Hannah's faithfulness to God—even through bitter disappointments.

All of a sudden, Lisa realized that if God was as loving, caring, and involved in her life as he had been in Hannah's, she could trust that his gifts and his timing were always the best. She could respond in worship and faithfulness, just like Hannah, instead of with the anxiety and doubt that had characterized her thoughts for so long. Because of the gospel, Lisa knew that God cared for her just as deeply as he had cared for Hannah. Because of the gospel she knew he could be trusted, and all because Estela was willing to share the seemingly obscure Old Testament story she had read that morning with Lisa. This new realization, and the worship that flowed from it, didn't end Lisa's struggle with anxiety, but it did help her take a significant step forward.

As we saw in chapter 11, in light of the reality of this broken world, we should invite those we love to lament. And as we saw in chapter 12, in light of the reality of the self-worship in our hearts, we should invite those we love to confess. In that same vein, in light of the reality of God's glorious grace in the gospel, we should invite those we love to remember.

Most of the time, the gospel truth that people most desperately need isn't truth they've never heard before, it's truth they've forgotten. It's truth that has fallen back in the recesses of their minds, pushed out by a litany of self-satisfying distractions. This is why they need to be invited to remember.

This tendency to forget comes naturally to us. Just a simple survey of biblical history demonstrates how quickly God's people tend to forget. This is why we all so desperately need to be reminded. Every single one of the Christians in your life needs to be reminded of gospel truth. But sometimes just reminding someone isn't quite enough. We need to do more than just speak the words they need to hear; we need to help grab their attention and invite them to remember.

Think about each of the people that you know God has called you to love. Every one of them is suffering in unique ways. Every one of them is sinning in unique ways. But they all have this one thing in common: every one of their souls is longing to remember gospel truth.

It makes me think of an old hymn. I like the slow pace of hymns. It reminds me of the pace genuine loving relationships require. This slow and rolling hymn gives voice to the longing of every soul you're ministering to. People may come to you with all sorts of different hurts or struggles, but, deep down, this is what their souls are begging you to do:

Tell me the old, old story,
Of unseen things above,
Of Jesus and His glory,
Of Jesus and His love.
Tell me the story simply,
As to a little child;
For I am weak and weary,
And helpless and defiled.

Tell me the story slowly,
That I may take it in—
That wonderful redemption,
God's remedy for sin.
Tell me the story often,
For I forget so soon;
The "early dew" of morning
Has passed away at noon.

Tell me the story softly,
With earnest tones and grave;
Remember I'm the sinner
Whom Jesus came to save.
Tell me the story always,
If you would really be,
In any time of trouble,
A comforter to me.[6]

ENDNOTES

1. Of all the resources I have referenced in this book, if you pick up only one, let it be this one: Milton Vincent, *A Gospel Primer for Christians*.
2. Vincent, *Gospel Primer for Christians*, 13.
3. Matt Chandler and Michael Snetzer, *Recovering Redemption*, 1–2.
4. D. A. Carson, *How Long, O Lord?*, 191.
5. Vincent, *Gospel Primer for Christians*, 30.
6. Poem by Katherine Hankey (1866).

CHAPTER 14

MORE THAN CHANGE

Gospeling, Part 4

Tony's relationship with painkillers had a long history. It had started, innocently enough, with a motorcycle accident. His doctor had prescribed him an opioid for his recovery process, providing him enough for his journey through physical therapy. While he tried to use it sparingly, his recovery lasted far longer than he expected. As a result, the prescription needed to be refilled a couple of times, and his body became awfully used to the effects. It was quite an ordeal when he finally had to wean himself off of it, but he did.

Even once his recovery was over, though, he continued to battle chronic back pain that never quite went away. He tried chiropractors, acupuncturists, and yoga, but nothing seemed to help. A couple of years later, a different doctor prescribed him a fentanyl patch to help cope with the pain. His body remembered the chemical, and it appreciated the reintroduction. This kicked off a two-year journey in which Tony's body seldom went without the drug. A number of times he also took more than had been pre-scribed and ended up either loopy or he completely passed out.

By the time we sat down together, Tony knew he had a problem. We met together through the various stages of physical withdrawal and addressed all of the issues of access. Tony communicated with his doctor, who helped him wean off the drug responsibly, and he cut off all ties with other users he knew. In addition, he allowed his roommate to hold his other medications for him (including Tylenol), in order to keep him from trying to abuse anything else. It wasn't an easy or painless process, but Tony was determined to kick this addiction that had slowly but surely taken over more and more of his life.

However, as I'm sure you can guess at this point in the book, Tony's addiction was deeper and more complex than even he realized. Tony had suffered in numerous ways that had contributed to his addiction. The pill-popping culture he grew up in, his overzealous pain doctors, and his genetic predisposition all contributed in significant ways to this mess. But so did his fear of discomfort, worship of efficiency, and desire to always be in control. There were all sorts of ways that Tony's self-worship had also fueled the predicament he found himself in.

As a result, Tony needed more than just help through the detox phase, or tools to keep him from relapsing. As helpful as those things were in the short term, what Tony ultimately needed was gospel truth. And as we explored the glories of the gospel together, Tony's heart began to soften, and his commitment to stay clean began to strengthen. One day he asked me a fascinating question. He said, "I know that I'm supposed to 'put off' using/abusing drugs. And I know we've spent a lot of time focusing on making sure I don't do that anymore. But what am I supposed to 'put on' instead? What's the opposite of abusing opioids?"

You see, to continue to grow and become more like Christ, Tony needed more than just gospel truths. He needed *more* than to be reminded of the magnitude of God's grace. Tony also needed to be reminded of how radical the call to follow Christ is. He needed to be shown the real, practical acts of obedience God was calling him to (beyond just stopping the drugs). Tony needed to be instructed in gospel commands.

Gospel Commands

Gospel commands are God's practical instructions for how to glorify him and reflect his character. They are the behaviors, thoughts, and emotions that are produced by a God-worshiping heart. As we are reminded of gospel truth, our hearts are inspired to worship God more and more. Gospel commands teach us *how* to glorify him and emulate him practically in our day-to-day lives.

The more I come to realize how spiritually rich I am, the more I should strive to live like it. The more glorious, gracious, and beautiful I realize God is, the more I should strive to honor him with everything I do, think, and feel. Worship is never just an internal reality; it always makes its way out into the day-to-day realities of our lives. When I am captivated by God, I can't help but long to please him. As Milton Vincent puts it, "Captured by his love . . . my smitten heart increasingly burns to do His will and feasts itself on doing so."[1]

So what is his will? If my heart increasingly burns to do his will, then it must be desperate to know what that will is. God's will, as revealed in his New Testament instructions, is what I'm calling "gospel commands." Jesus sums up all of his gospel commands in two very simple, yet impossibly difficult, instructions: "You shall love the Lord your God with all your heart and with all your soul and with all your mind. This is the great and first commandment. And a second is like it: You shall love your neighbor as yourself" (Matt. 22:37–39).

Love God and love others. This is the most basic summary of how we are called to live as new creations in Christ. While these two simple commandments encapsulate every part of the Christian life, there is still more we need to know. We need directions about *how* to love God. We need instructions on *how* to love others. Because of our history as ardent self-worshipers, and because of the residual self-worship still at work in our hearts, loving God and loving others doesn't come all that naturally to us.

Therefore, we need help understanding how our behaviors, thoughts, and emotions can glorify God and bless our neighbor. This is why God provides so many practical instructions in the New Testament. He doesn't give us these gospel commands as ways for us to earn our salvation or prove our worth. He has already completely saved us and declared us unimaginably worthy in Christ. He's given us gospel commands so that when our hearts long to worship him and do his will, we might know what that will is. Our souls long to be reminded of gospel truth. And as that gospel truth takes root, they will similarly long to be instructed in gospel commands.

THE CALL TO TRUST

The greatest way we can express our love for God in our thoughts and emotions is to trust him, especially in the midst of suffering. Trust conveys a deep level of familiarity, love, and respect. Think about what it communicates when a child doesn't trust their parent. Either the parent is untrustworthy, or the relationship has somehow been broken, or both. When we don't trust God, we are similarly conveying either his untrustworthiness, or the brokenness of our relationship with him, or both. However, because of the gospel, we can know that we have a God who is completely trustworthy and a relationship that has been completely restored. As a result, it is only natural that he would expect us to trust him.

Of course, trust isn't easy, and it's not something you can just will into being. Many of us find trusting God extremely difficult, especially when we're caught in the deluge of life's pain. But things that are impossible on our own are made possible with God. The God who parted the Red Sea, brought manna down from heaven, and raised Jesus from the grave can grow trust in even the most fearful hearts. And he does it through reminders of gospel truth.

Just before his call to "set your hope fully on [God's] grace" (1 Peter 1:13), Peter explains that it is reminders of gospel truth that fuel this trust—and its emotional manifestation, joy:

*Blessed be the God and Father of our Lord Jesus
Christ! According to his great mercy, he has caused
us to be born again to a living hope through the
resurrection of Jesus Christ from the dead, to an
inheritance that is imperishable, undefiled, and
unfading, kept in heaven for you, who by God's
power are being guarded through faith for a
salvation ready to be revealed in the last time. In
this you rejoice, though now for a little while, if
necessary, you have been grieved by various trials,
so that the tested genuineness of your faith—more
precious than gold that perishes though it is tested
by fire—may be found to result in praise and glory
and honor at the revelation of Jesus Christ.*

(1 Peter 1:3–7)

The first few verses of 1 Peter sure sound a lot like the
first few verses of Ephesians, don't they? Peter lists a number
of our spiritual blessings and then calls us to rejoice in those
spiritual blessings—even in the midst of suffering! Whatever
your "various trials" might be, you can trust God—and you can
rejoice—because of who he is and what he has done for you. You
can rejoice in the fact that he is redeeming those trials for your
good and for his glory. To the extent that your heart is longing to
worship him and do his will, you can know that his will is that
you would trust him and rejoice.

The same is true not just in our suffering, but also in our *fear* of
suffering. It may not be a financial crisis, but a *potential* financial
crisis. It may not be a health scare, but a *potential* health scare. It
may not be a family issue, but a *potential* family issue. How are we
called to honor God when there are so many unknowns?

We hear both from the pen of Paul and the lips of Jesus the
call to "not be anxious about anything" (Phil. 4:6; Matt. 6:25–34).
Yet our hearts are often consumed with fear and anxiety. The
future is so uncertain. The darkness of this world is so real. We
have so little control. How could we possibly not be anxious? It
would take a supernatural work of God!

But a supernatural work is exactly what he has done. He has inserted light into the darkness. He has affirmed his absolute sovereignty. He has proven the goodness of his plans for the future. Gospel truth changes everything. So how can we demonstrate our love for such a good and gracious God? Again, by trusting him. By taking our anxious thoughts captive (2 Cor. 10:5) and giving them to him. "Humble yourselves, therefore, under the mighty hand of God so that at the proper time he may exalt you, casting all your anxieties on him, because he cares for you" (1 Peter 5:6–7).

When our hearts long to know how we can please God and do his will, one of his primary answers is simply: Trust me. Rejoice in me. Rest in me. Be secure in me. And, as we strive to honor this call, the main way this trust manifests itself is through our redeemed thoughts and emotions. "Saying emotions are redeemed is not to say that Christians are only happy. Rather it is to say that their emotional lives more closely reflect the values of God. . . . Depression is injected with joy, fear is cut through with peace, anger is blunted by patience."[2]

As you walk through Scripture, you will find emotional words like "joy" and "anxious" all over the place. I'm afraid that people are often confused at the thought of being instructed to feel an emotion. And yet, as our hearts are more and more captivated by the grace and glory of God, it makes more and more sense. We begin to realize that we are capable of internal thoughts and emotions that we may never have thought possible before. We realize that trust-fueled thoughts and emotions are the natural byproduct of our increasingly God-worshiping hearts.

THE CALL TO OBEY

While the greatest way we can express our love for God in our thoughts and emotions is to trust him, the greatest way we can express our love for God in our thoughts and behaviors is to obey him. Obedience is an unpopular concept in most circles today because autonomy and self-governance are two of our culture's highest values. Similar to trust, genuine obedience conveys a deep level of honor, love, and respect. Again, a parent and child provide a helpful analogy. Think about what it communicates when a child doesn't obey their parent. There is a lack of respect, a lack of honor, and a prioritization of the child's desires over the desires of the one in authority. Kids are natural self-worshipers.

But as the gospel takes deeper and deeper root in our hearts, and we come to worship God more and more, it is only natural that our self-worshiping disobedience will be replaced by loving obedience to our perfect Savior. It's for this reason, in fact, that Scripture clearly equates love for God with obedience: "By this we know that we love the children of God, when we love God and obey his commandments. For this is the love of God, that we keep his commandments. And his commandments are not burdensome" (1 John 5:2–3).

Wait, his commandments are not burdensome? How can doing what someone else wants instead of following your own desires not be a burden? This is only possible if we are truly being transformed from the inside out. Think back to all the incredible spiritual blessings we looked at from Ephesians 1–3. How does your understanding of yourself change when you realize that *that* is your true identity? Again, as we come to understand how spiritually rich we are in Christ, our souls will long for our entire lives to reflect that reality. This is exactly what Paul wanted for the Ephesians, too. He wanted them to live outward lives that reflected the inward reality: "I therefore, a prisoner for the Lord, urge you to walk in a manner worthy of the calling to which you have been called" (Eph. 4:1).

And to help them "walk in a manner worthy of the calling to which [they had] been called" Paul went on to give them (and us!) gospel commands:

> . . . assuming that you have heard about him and were taught in him, as the truth is in Jesus, to put off your old self, which belongs to your former manner of life and is corrupt through deceitful desires, and to be renewed in the spirit of your minds, and to put on the new self, created after the likeness of God in true righteousness and holiness.
> (Eph. 4:21–24)

We talked about the process of being "renewed in the spirit of your minds" in the last chapter, but what specifically are we called to "put off" and "put on"? How can we live this genuinely God-honoring life our souls long to live? Throughout the rest of Ephesians, Paul answers these questions with a whole host of different gospel commands. Here's a sampling just from chapter 4:

PUT OFF

- Callousness (4:19)
- Sensuality (4:19)
- Greed (4:19)
- Every kind of impurity (4:19)
- Falsehood (4:25)
- Sinful anger (4:26, 31)
- Stealing (4:28)
- Corrupting talk (4:29)
- Bitterness (4:31)
- Wrath (4:31)
- Clamor (4:31)
- Slander (4:31)
- Malice (4:31)

PUT ON

- Humility (4:2)
- Gentleness (4:2)
- Patience (4:2)
- Bearing with others (4:2)
- Maintaining unity (4:3)
- Truth-speaking (4:15, 25)
- Honest work (4:28)
- Giving (4:28)
- Speech that builds up (4:29)
- Speech that fits the occasion (4:29)
- Speech that gives grace (4:29)
- Kindness (4:32)
- Tenderheartedness (4:32)
- Forgiveness (4:32)

This doesn't even include the specific gospel commands Paul provides for marriage (5:22–33), parenting (6:1–4), and employment (6:5–9)![3] We only have to take a quick look at this list to see that God is calling us to a serious and radical obedience. He's not interested in tweaking our habits or making a few improvements around the edges; he's calling us to obedience in every area of our lives. Of course, none of us have arrived yet. But he's calling us to continue to grow in obedience—to pursue *radical* obedience—for the sake of his glory. He wants to shape the way we work, the way we talk, the way we drive, and even the way we eat (1 Cor. 10:31).

God's calling us to flee sexual immorality (1 Cor. 6:18). He's calling us to be constant in prayer (Rom. 12:12). He's calling us to consider others more significant than ourselves (Phil. 2:3). He's calling us to be generous and ready to share (1 Tim. 6:18). And all because "we are his workmanship, created in Christ Jesus for good works" (Eph. 2:10).

The call to obey gospel commands isn't a broad, general call. It's a specific call with countless specific instructions scattered throughout the New Testament. All these specific commands aren't meant to overwhelm us or scare us. They are simply another product of God's grace. They graciously tell us how we can worship God and live a life consistent with who we are in Christ. They graciously detail how God has designed life to be lived, and how we can flourish for his glory and our own good. This kind of radical obedience isn't just what the "serious Christians" are called to pursue; it's the life that every person who has been transformed by the gospel is called to pursue. It's the sweet fruit of a tree whose roots have been made new.

THE GOAL: CHRISTLIKENESS

As God-worship displaces self-worship in our hearts, we should expect it to transform the way we think, feel, and act. But this doesn't happen all at once. In fact, we'll spend our entire lives continuing to become (in practice) who we are (in Christ). But this means that, for the entirety of our lives as Christians, our thoughts, emotions, and behaviors will constantly be changing. They'll increasingly reflect Christ's thoughts, emotions, and behaviors. And, if you remember, this has been the goal all along: to become more like Christ.

As I mentioned back in chapter 2, people have all sorts of different goals in the midst of the messes in their lives. Sometimes, they just want the suffering to go away. Sometimes, they want to be able to hold on to that last little bit of sin without being weighed down by guilt. Sometimes, they simply want to wallow in the mess of it all. But God has a higher goal. He has a higher purpose for the messes in each one of our lives. He wants to use them to shape us more and more into the image of his Son. In the last chapter we looked at God's promise in Romans 8 that he will work all things (including our messes) together for our ultimate good. Paul immediately goes on to define what our ultimate good is: "And we know that for those who love God all things work together for good, for those who are called according to his purpose. For those whom he foreknew he also predestined to be *conformed to the image of his Son,* in order that he might be the firstborn among many brothers" (Rom. 8:28–29).

Our ultimate good is that we would grow to trust like Christ. In the garden of Gethsemane, Jesus trusted the Father in the face of the greatest suffering ever experienced on earth (Matt. 26:36–42). He knew what lay ahead, and he wanted to avoid it if at all possible. Yet he trusted his Father. Jesus trusted God the Father as he was led, not around that suffering, but through it.

Our ultimate good is that we would grow to obey like Christ. When Satan tempted Jesus, the temptation he felt was very real (Matt. 4:1–11). When he was offered food, he hadn't eaten for forty days. The hunger he experienced must have been overwhelming, yet he obeyed. When he was offered every kingdom on earth, and all their glory, he had been without the glory he deserved for thirty years. The longing to receive even a piece of the power and glory he had possessed from eternity past must have been consuming, yet he obeyed.

The call to trust and obey is not just a call to come under the authority of God (although it is that); it's also—most fundamentally—a call to become like Christ. As his image-bearers, this is what we were designed for. We were created to reflect God's image and manifest his likeness. But, because of the fall, that likeness has been scuffed and marred. That is why, in Christ, we have now been re-created to reflect that image again. We are being transformed into the image we once were (in Adam and Eve) and have been made into (in Christ). "And we all, with unveiled face, beholding the glory of the Lord, are being transformed into the same image from one degree of glory to another. For this comes from the Lord who is the Spirit" (2 Cor. 3:18).

This call to live a transformed life is a call that can only be fulfilled by the power of the Spirit. Every act of trust and obedience we are called to isn't, most basically, the fruit of a strong will or even the fruit of gospel care. It's the fruit of the Spirit. Love, joy, peace, patience, kindness, goodness, faithfulness, gentleness, and self-control are all produced by the work of the Spirit in our lives (Gal. 5:22–23). If we are going to become more like Jesus, we need the Spirit to empower that supernatural transformation.

And yet, love (Matt. 22:39), joy (Phil. 4:4), peace (Matt. 6:25), patience (Rom. 12:12), kindness (Eph. 4:32), goodness (1 Tim. 4:12), faithfulness (1 Tim. 6:11), gentleness (Titus 3:2), and self-control (1 Peter 4:7) are also all gospel commands. They are practical instructions that we are to put effort—significant effort—into following. So which is it? Is our transformation into Christlikeness something the Spirit does, or something we do? Are our trust and obedience a work of God or our own responsibility? The short answer is: both.

Jerry Bridges provides a great illustration to help us understand this potential paradox.

A farmer plows his field, sows the seed, and fertilizes and cultivates—all the while knowing that in the final analysis he is utterly dependent on forces outside of himself. He knows he cannot cause the seed to germinate, nor can he produce the rain and sunshine for growing and harvesting the crop. For a successful harvest, he is dependent on these things from God.

Yet the farmer knows that unless he diligently pursues his responsibilities to plow, plant, fertilize, and cultivate, he cannot expect a harvest at the end of the season. In a sense he is in a partnership with God, and he will reap its benefits only when he has fulfilled his own responsibilities.

> *Farming is a joint venture between God and the farmer.*
> *The farmer cannot do what God must do, and God will not*
> *do what the farmer should do. We can say just as accurately*
> *that the pursuit of holiness is a joint venture between God*
> *and the Christian.*[4]

Just like the farmer, when it comes to growing in Christlikeness you cannot do what God must do, but God will not do what you should do. God will grant you supernatural power through his Spirit, but you must still do the hard work of trusting and obeying in order to become more like Christ.

INSTRUCTING IN GOSPEL COMMANDS

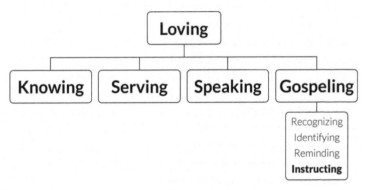

If the goal of our lives is to glorify God by becoming more and more like Christ, then the ultimate goal of gospel care must be to help others become more like Christ as well. Therefore, gospel care that is truly loving cannot stop short of instructing those we're ministering to in specific gospel commands.

This is the final step of what it means to "gospel" another person. Gospeling is not only helping people see that their problems are worse than they realized, and that God's grace is greater than they've ever imagined. It also, necessarily, involves helping them see that, in light of that grace, they are called to live lives of trust and obedience more radical than they ever thought possible.

As we've walked through each component of "gospeling," each step has come with an invitation. As we recognize the depths of our fallen world, we invite those we love to lament. As we identify the depths of their fallen hearts, we invite those we love to confess. As we remind those we love of gospel truth, we invite them to remember. And, finally, as we instruct those we love in gospel commands, we invite them to repent.

When you hear the word "repent," what comes to mind? I'm afraid that most of us think of a large sign on the end of a stick being held by an angry mob as they yell "Repent!" at passersby. That kind of out-of-touch, hateful interaction is the exact opposite of what Scripture calls us to. It is the antithesis of gospel care. However, instead of abandoning the word "repent" because of the way it has sometimes been abused, I think it's important that we reclaim it.

"Repent" is a word that was repeatedly on Jesus' lips, and it's the word Peter used to tell the crowd at Pentecost how they could be saved (Acts 2:38). When Paul was instructing the Corinthians in gospel commands, it was repentance that he said he was after (2 Cor. 7:8–10). In the same way, whenever you call someone to trust or obey Christ in practical ways, you are calling them to repent.

Repentance is being so overwhelmed by the glory of God's grace that you turn from your self-worship and strive to worship God with your whole life. As you provide gospel care to people in the midst of their mess, genuine love calls them to repent. It reminds them of gospel truth and then calls them to respond to that truth in trust and obedience.

As we've seen, the New Testament is filled with specific commands. It's filled with emotion commands. It's filled with thought commands. It's filled with behavior commands. Our job is to identify which of those commands are the most important and most pressing in a given situation and call those we love to repent.

But as we wrap up this chapter—and this section, and, in fact, the entire book—it's important for you to recognize where your responsibility stops and where the responsibility of the person you're ministering to begins. Calling someone to repent is your job (as you gospel them). But the repentance itself isn't your responsibility; it's theirs. You can call someone to repent, but you can't repent for them. The old saying about horses and water and drinking holds true.

Think back to Tony. I said that Tony needed help identifying what, specifically, God was asking of him—beyond just stopping the drugs. But while identifying specific acts of obedience was something I could do for Tony, the actual living out of those acts wasn't. Tony needed to repent, and he needed to repent of more than just the drug abuse that had become the headline problem in his life.

I've found that a helpful illustration comes from simply asking the question: "When is a thief no longer a thief?" In other words: How does a thief know when he has truly transformed? Of course, the most immediate answer people give is, "When he stops stealing!" The problem is, a thief could stop stealing for all sorts of different reasons. Maybe he's locked up in jail and doesn't have the opportunity. Maybe he's been caught twice already and he's afraid of getting his third strike. Maybe his mom no longer leaves her purse out in the open, and he hasn't developed the creativity to look anywhere else yet. Any of these are plausible reasons why a thief might stop stealing, but none of them mean he's transformed. However, Ephesians 4 provides our answer: "Let the thief no longer steal, but rather let him labor, doing honest work with his own hands, so that he may have something to share with anyone in need" (Eph. 4:28).

You know that a thief is no longer a thief when his heart has been so radically transformed by the gospel that he not only stops stealing (puts off), but he actually works a job, does honest work, and gives to others what he used to take from them (puts on).

In the same way, Tony hadn't necessarily transformed simply because he stopped taking opioids. There were all sorts of different alternative idols that could have motivated that. He could have stopped taking opioids because his prescription ran out and he was too afraid to find an illegal dealer. He could have stopped because he wanted a job that required drug tests. He could have stopped because, otherwise, his fiancée wouldn't marry him.

But, for Tony, God was calling him to more than just put an end to his drug abuse. God was also calling him to begin serving his fiancée sacrificially, to begin combatting his pain with patience and prayer, to begin pursuing others in the church out of love, and to begin practicing self-control in his eating and online gaming, too.

Those weren't things I could do for Tony. Those were choices he had to make for himself. My job was to help him realize that the problem was worse than he knew, that God's grace was greater than he imagined, and that God's call was more radical than he ever thought possible. My job was to instruct him in the clear gospel commands that God was calling him to trust and obey. My job was to gospel him. And—even more fundamentally—my job was to love him.

ENDNOTES

1. Milton Vincent, *A Gospel Primer for Christians*, 29.
2. Jeremy Pierre, *The Dynamic Heart in Daily Life*, 83, 82.
3. This is a good opportunity to notice that, if the gospel commands for specific relationships located in the latter part of this letter are just that—gospel commands—then we shouldn't even begin to try to instruct people with these passages (in order to help their marriages, homes, or workplaces) until we have first spent time saturating them in gospel truths. Too often, Ephesians 5 gets treated like "God's tips for a healthy marriage" instead of God's description of how a life that has been transformed by the gospel should look in the context of marriage.
4. Jerry Bridges, *The Pursuit of Holiness*, 11–12.

CHAPTER 15

THE SIMPLICITY OF UNSCRIPTED LOVE

You may have noticed that none of the stories throughout this book have a conclusion. None of them were tied up with a nice, neat bow. None of them were given a "happily ever after" ending. You may feel frustrated by that. You may want to know what happened to Tony, Ben and Lucy, Arash and Leila, or Jessica. Maybe you want to know because you like stories with a happy ending. Maybe you want to know because you want "proof" that gospel care "works." Maybe you want to know because you know someone in a similar situation. But that's not what this book is about.

This book isn't about guaranteeing happy endings (at least in this life). It isn't about a system that produces magical results. It isn't a handbook for how to de-mess your friends. It's about how God is calling you to love others in the midst of the mess, regardless of the outcomes.

Almost all of the people whose stories I've shared *are* continuing to grow and become more like Christ. Many of them have moved on from the messes I've described—and are now learning to navigate different messes in their lives. But not all of them. A few are still really struggling. And a number, while they *have* become more like Jesus, are still on the journey through their same mess.

That's what ministering to people is like. It's messy, unpredictable, and doesn't have a storybook ending. Since we're not God, we don't get to see the whole picture. We only get a glimpse of a moment. We ride the roller coaster along with those we're ministering to. And as we care for them in the midst of *their* messes, we have to navigate the dynamics of our own messes as well.

If we assume we're responsible for more than we are, caring for others becomes a burden that quickly leads to burnout. If we assume that our own faithfulness is measured by someone else's trust or obedience, we will constantly be discouraged and confused. Just because someone turns away from God doesn't mean you have failed them as a friend. And just because someone has been transformed doesn't mean you are the hero of the story.

That's why we need to constantly remember what our responsibility *is* before God, and what it is not. We need to remember that Scripture doesn't call us to fix people or magically make their messes disappear. Scripture doesn't call us to manufacture someone else's trust and obedience. Scripture doesn't call us to be anyone's savior—because they already have one.

However, there are a number of things that Scripture *does* call us to. And *that's* what this book has been about. This book isn't about what *others* are called to do; this book is about what *you're* called to do. And what you are called to is the art of gospel care.

Gospel Care

Gospel care is the God-exalting, grace-saturated art of loving another person, through patiently knowing, sacrificially serving, truthfully speaking, and consistently applying the gospel in order to help them become more like Jesus.

I hope this definition means a lot more to you now than it did when I first shared it back in chapter 2. Since then, we have walked through each one of these categories and unpacked seventeen practical ways we are called to love others. Looking at it all together it sure looks like a lot! How are you supposed to remember all of that? Should you draw this diagram on your hand or something?

This is why I have summarized everything we're called to do in these four simple categories: knowing, serving, speaking, and gospeling. When it comes to ministering to others in the midst of the mess, God is simply calling you to love them by knowing them, serving them, speaking to them, and gospeling them. You can remember that! Especially since you're doing most of it already.

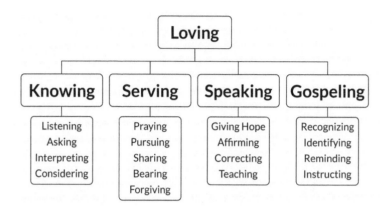

You already know your friends pretty well. Just knowing that they're in a mess at all means you're well on your way. You've listened and asked questions, and you just need to keep doing more of the same. Ask intentional questions, and listen patiently for the answers. Take time to really think and pray about what they've shared and what they might need. That's really all it takes.

I'm sure you're already serving your friends in a number of ways, too. Maybe it's some practical help here and there, or simply taking the time to pray for them. Just the fact that you have relationships at all means you're bearing with people and forgiving them to some degree—unless you've found some already perfected friends. You just need to keep looking for more and more ways in which you can practically serve them. How can you convey your love for them in tangible ways that might surprise them or bless them?

You're probably well on your way to speaking truth to your friends as well. Whether it's in a text, at a park, over email, or in your family room, I'm sure you spend time talking with your friends one way or another. And I'm sure there have been ways in which you have affirmed them, taught them, or corrected them along the way. Now you have the opportunity to be even more intentional with what you say. How could your friends use some hope, correction, or affirmation today?

You may even be gospeling others already, even if you wouldn't have called it that. But perhaps you aren't quite yet. Maybe you never realized how pervasive the problem of suffering is or how deep the problem of sin goes. Maybe you don't usually think about how great and glorious the gospel is. Maybe the idea of calling your friends to repent has seemed awkward or uncomfortable. Well, now's the time to start!

If you know the gospel at all, you know enough to speak gospel truth to those around you. Remember, most of the time the people around you don't need to be taught gospel truth; they just need to be reminded of it. That means that, even if you've only been a Christian for a few months, you still know gospel truths that your pastor, your community group leader, and every one of your friends desperately need to be reminded of every day. If you've read any portion of the New Testament, chances are you've come across all sorts of gospel commands that those around you should also be called to trust and obey.

I've used a lot of words to unpack these concepts over the past fourteen chapters, but the truth is: it's not that complicated. Gospel care is something anyone can do. Because gospel care is something every Christian is called to do.

UNSCRIPTED LOVE

So, where are you going to start? Who in your life needs gospel care? I know that there are messes all around you. You have friends that are struggling with their kids or with their parents. You have friends that are addicted to alcohol or to porn. You have friends that are slogging through depression or fighting through chronic pain. You have friends that are battling their eating habits or are miserable at their jobs. I know you have friends—and I know they have messes. And, now that you've read this book, you know that you're called to minister to them in the midst of the mess.

Just remember, there's no script. Gospel care isn't like playing a fully orchestrated piece of music with every note in its proper place and every twist and turn predetermined. Gospel care is like jazz. It's fluid, unpredictable, surprising, and unique every time. For all the years that I've spent discipling and counseling others, I have never once had the same conversation twice. I've preached the same sermon more than once, I've taught the same class more than once, but I have never, in my entire life, had the same personal conversation more than once.

That's because personal ministry is unscripted. There's no specific Bible verse that always fits for "depression" or "stress" or "relationship problems." There's no set amount of time you should listen and ask questions before you speak up. There's no right number of gospel truths you should cover before moving on to gospel commands.

Even the structure we've gone through in this book provides more of a musical key than it does a formal score. The key of a song tells you what notes go appropriately together. It gives you the standard notes you can play for the song to remain in harmony. But the key doesn't tell you which notes to play when. And it doesn't tell you what order to play everything in.

That's how you should think of all the topics we've covered in this book. Of course, some components have a logical progression to them—listening should usually come before speaking; gospel truth should usually come before gospel commands. But the reality is that every different situation requires the different components of gospel care in a different order. You'll spend time knowing, then gospeling, then serving, then knowing, then speaking, and then knowing again. Or not. Every relationship, and every season in every relationship, will be unique.

Therefore, you don't need a script. In fact, if you try to use a script, it will only make things worse. No one likes to be cared for via a formula. You can't do gospel care by equation. It's impersonal and lazy. It feels formal and forced. It doesn't build relationships; it breaks them down. It's the antithesis of love. And love—well, the Beatles were right: love is all you need.

If you have come to know God's love through the gospel, you have everything you need to begin ministering to those around you in the midst of the mess. There are plenty of ways you can continue to grow, but to get started all you need is the Spirit of God in your soul and the Word of God in your heart. You don't need to muster up your own love (because you can't). You simply need to be reminded of the magnitude of *his* love. Your own heart needs to be captivated again by the beauty and glory of God's grace. *You* need some gospel truth.

In this the love of God was made manifest among us, that God sent his only Son into the world, so that we might live through him. In this is love, not that we have loved God but that he loved us and sent his Son to be the propitiation for our sins. Beloved, if God so loved us, we also ought to love one another.

(1 John 4:9–11)

As I bring this book to a close, here is the simple gospel command I want to leave you with: love one another. Again, don't be overwhelmed by all the different ways you *could* love those around you. Simply ask God to help you see the simple, practical ways in which you *should* love those around you.

Who around you is hurting? Who is struggling? What are the messes you already know about? Start with just one person. Take the time to prayerfully consider: What does this person need most right now? Should I take time to know them? Is there a way I should serve them? Is there truth I should speak to them? Should I take time to gospel them?

You may not know exactly what they need, and you may not be sure what you have to offer. But you can know this: God wants you to play some part in their story.

ACKNOWLEDGMENTS

The number of people God has used to play a part in my own messy story, and in the story of the development of this book, is innumerable. To all those who have, in one way or another, helped me to become more like Jesus in the midst of my own mess, this book contains within it the legacy of your faithfulness and love. Similarly, to all those who I have had the honor of teaching and ministering to over the past decade and a half, each one of you have contributed to these insights, as you have repeatedly given me the privilege of having a front row seat to watch God work in your lives.

There are also a number of people I would be remiss if I did not specifically acknowledge for the ways they contributed to the development of this book in significant and sacrificial ways. First, I am overwhelmingly grateful for the gift of my brothers (John and Jeff). I am particularly thankful for the night, four years ago, they looked me in the eye and told me that I needed to write this book, as well as the countless moments of encouragement they've provided throughout this process.

It is the privilege of my life to pastor the church where God has so graciously placed our family. The co-pastors (vocational and non-vocational) with whom I have labored have been an incredible encouragement, and each one of them has helped shape the content of this book through various conversations and as they live out its principles faithfully among our spiritual family. I am more thankful than I can say for Bill, Jim, José, Reggie, Ara, Brian, Chris, Zach, Matt, Jason, and Dustin. Matt has been a particularly helpful editor and reviewer over the years that this content has been developed. In addition, it must be acknowledged that the quality of writing throughout this book is due in large part to the careful and faithful editing that Brian, in particular, has provided. He has helped to clarify my teaching voice for fourteen years, and his fingerprints are on every page of this book both editorially and personally.

It is a similarly unique privilege to get to work with the incredible church staff God has built at Cornerstone West L.A. I'm more thankful than they will ever know for not only their editorial help in reviewing the manuscript, but also their constant friendship. The edits provided by Ashley L, Ashley R, Kirsten, Danny, Jeremy, Reggie, Valerie, Jim, Becky, and Amy, have made this book much more accessible than it otherwise would have been. In addition, I continue to thank God for Amy's constant help in scheduling, brainstorming, and editing that have made the completion of this book possible.

In addition, I have come to be more thankful that I ever expected for the support of Shepherd Press throughout this process and for their willingness to join up with an unknown local church pastor because they believed in the importance of a resource like this. I'm thankful for the support of Aaron Tripp and the editing of Suzanne Mitchell. And I am particularly grateful for the insightful editing and steady, wise, and compassionate guidance of Jim Holmes who has become a dear friend and confidant throughout the process.

I am also deeply indebted to the dozens of friends who have given me permission to use versions of their stories (with names and details altered) to demonstrate how God's Word and his body work powerfully in the context of relationships. I am humbled that they would not only allow me to be a part of the messier moments of their stories, but that they would also generously allow me to share those moments with so many others.

In addition, Jacy Corral (a dear friend and amazing children's book author/illustrator!) has brought the key concepts in the book to life through her simple and beautiful diagrams. And she has also provided the great artwork for the cover. Her generosity and collaboration are a true blessing.

Finally, I continually thank God for Harper, Addison, Lincoln, and Skylar, and for their continued patience with a messy dad. I am especially grateful for the constant encouragement they provided, especially during the most intense writing weeks.

And, of course no list of thanks would be complete without mentioning my favorite editor of all, my wife Lara. She has pored over these chapters more than anyone, and has helped to shape not only the words on the page, but the life those words pour forth from. Her support and love in every facet of life is the greatest gift I have ever received apart from salvation. She embodies the love described throughout these chapters, and no one else in the world has so graciously and consistently helped me become more like Jesus.

All of this thanks is, ultimately, a recognition of the immense and unimaginable nature of God's grace. The gift of Christ alone would have been more than I could ever have imagined, and yet his blessings continue to abound. In the midst of my mess, his love is never ending, his grace is never ceasing, and his faithfulness is never failing. It is through this love that he continues to make me, more and more, into the image of Christ. My prayer is simply that, through this book, every reader might know this love more deeply and, as a result, continue to be transformed more completely.

Go deeper with study videos from the

Intro to Messy Care
& Discipleship

The IBCD Intro to (Messy) Care and Discipleship is made up of eight teaching sessions designed to equip small groups to engage in one-another gospel care. Eight roundtable discussions follow each of the teaching sessions, and a companion Study Guide is designed to complement the video resources.

This program expands on the content of *Loving Messy People* and demonstrates how every Christian can be used by God to care for the hurting and struggling people around them. The discussions are strategically comprised of a diverse collection of pastors, advocates, small group leaders, biblical counselors, and disciplers. They provide an opportunity to learn from the experience of real people who are loving others in the real messes of life.

The corresponding Study Guide, by Scott Mehl and the IBCD team, is filled with a treasure trove of real-life case studies, application questions, prompts for further Bible study, and assignments to put the principles discussed into practice. This guide is a great resource that can be used individually, in a small group, or in a Sunday school setting.

Learn more at ibcd.org/messy

COUNSELING ONE ANOTHER:
A THEOLOGY OF INTERPERSONAL DISCIPLESHIP

Paul Tautges
Trade paperback, 192pp
ISBN: 978-1-63342-094-6

A book to help believers understand the process of being transformed by God's grace and truth

"*This book gets it right! Comprehensive and convincing,* Counseling One Another *shows how true biblical counseling and preaching fit hand-in-glove. Those who preach, teach or counsel regularly are sure to benefit greatly from this helpful resource.*"
—*Dr. John MacArthur, Pastor-Teacher,*
Grace Community Church;
President, The Master's University and Seminary

"*Paul Tautges lays the theological foundation for biblical counseling— in a way that is both comprehensive and compassionate. This book demonstrates a staunch commitment to an expository, exegetical examination of counseling as presented in God's Word. Any pastor or lay person wanting a foundational starting point for understanding Christ-centered, comprehensive, and compassionate biblical counseling in the local church would be wise to read and reread* Counseling One Another.*"
—*Bob Kellemen,*
Executive Director of The Biblical Counseling Coalition

Counsel with Confidence:
A Quick Reference Guide
for Biblical Counselors and Disciplers

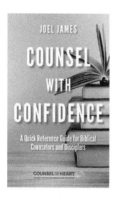

Joel James
Trade paperback, 224pp
ISBN: 978-1-63342-148-6

When you were learning to ride a bicycle, the hardest part was the first few pedal strokes—those wobbly seconds before you built up enough momentum to maintain your balance. A generous push from your dad was just what you needed to avoid ending up in a heap of elbows, knees, handlebars, and spokes. Counseling is similar. Sometimes you need something to give you some momentum, something to give you the confidence that you're on the right track. If you've ever felt like that, this book is for you.

Author Joel James has an M.Div. and a D.Min. from The Master's Seminary and is the pastor-teacher of Grace Fellowship in Pretoria, South Africa. He and his wife, Ruth, have been married since 1993 and have two children.

About Shepherd Press Publications

- They are gospel driven.
- They are heart focused.
- They are life changing.

Our Invitation to You

We passionately believe that what we are publishing can be of benefit to you, your family, your friends, and your work colleagues. So we are inviting you to join our online mailing list so that we may reach out to you with news about our latest and forthcoming publications, and with special offers.

Visit:

www.shepherdpress.com/newsletter

and provide your name and email address.